MULTILINGUAL MATTERS 85
Series Editor: Derrick Sharp

Linguistic and Communicative Competence: Topics in ESL

Christina Bratt Paulston

MULTILINGUAL MATTERS LTD
Clevedon • Philadelphia • Adelaide

Library of Congress Cataloging in Publication Data

Paulston, Christina Bratt, 1932-
Linguistic and Communicative Competence: Topics in ESL
p. cm. (Multilingual Matters: 85)
Includes bibliographical references and index
1. English language—Study and teaching—Foreign speakers. 2. Intercultural
communication. 3. Applied linguistics.
I. Title. II. Series: Multilingual Matters (Series): 85.
PE1128.A2P335   1992
428'.007   dc 20a

British Library Cataloguing in Publication Data

A CIP catalogue record for this book is available from the British Library.

ISBN 1-85359-149-1 (hbk)
ISBN 1-85359-148-3 (pbk)

Multilingual Matters Ltd

UK: Frankfurt Lodge, Clevedon Hall, Victoria Road, Clevedon, Avon BS21 7SJ.
USA: 1900 Frost Road, Suite 101, Bristol, PA 19007, USA.
Australia: P.O. Box 6025, 83 Gilles Street, Adelaide, SA 5000, Australia.

Printed and bound in Great Britain by the Longdunn Press, Bristol.

Contents

Sources

Introduction: English Teaching as a Foreign or Second Language. From: *The International Encyclopaedia of Education,* Oxford: Pergamon Press, 1985.

Chapter 1: On Creativity and Teaching. From *Teachers College Record,* 69 (4), 1968. Reprinted by permission.

Chapter 2: The Sequencing of Structural Pattern Drills. From *TESOL Quarterly,* September 1971. Reprinted by permission of TESOL, Inc.

Chapter 3: The Use of Video-tape in the Training of Foreign Language Teachers. From *Audio-Visual Instruction,* April 1972.

Chapter 4: Teaching the Culturally Different Pupil. School District of the City of Allentown, PA, 1973.

Chapter 5: Linguistic and Communicative Competence. From *TESOL Quarterly,* December 1974. Reprinted by permission of TESOL, Inc.

Chapter 6: Developing Communicative Competence: Goals, Procedures and Techniques. Washington, DC: TESOL Headquarters, September 1974.

Chapter 7: Comments on P. L. Hartman and E. L. Judd's *Sexism and TESOL Materials.* From *TESOL Quarterly,* 13 (2), 1979. Reprinted by permission of TESOL Inc.

Chapter 8: Notional Syllabuses Revisited: Some Comments. From *Applied Linguistics,* 11 (1), 1981. Reprinted by permission of Oxford University Press.

Chapter 9: Applied Linguistics: The Use of Linguistics in ESL. From *English as a Second Language* (ed. I. Feigenbaum), Arlington, TX: University of Texas Press, 1984. Reprinted by permission.

Chapter 10: Communicative Competence and Language Teaching: Second Thoughts. From *Communicative Language Teaching* (ed. F. K. Das), Singapore: RELC and Singapore University Press, 1984. Reprinted by permission.

Chapter 11: Linguistic Interaction, Intercultural Communication and Communicative Language Teaching. From *Intercultural Communication: What it Means to Chinese Learners in English* (ed. W. Hu), Shanghai: Shanghai Translation Publishing House, 1987.

Chapter 12: ESL in Bilingual Education. From *Festschrift for Joshua Fishman, Vol. I: Focus on Bilingual Education* (ed. O. Garcia), Amsterdam: John Benjamins, 1991. Reprinted by permission of John Benjamins Publishing Company.

Preface

Ever since I can remember, I have wanted to be a teacher. I recall a job orientation session at my high school in Stockholm in which I told the assembled group that I wanted to be a teacher of Swedish and rector for a *gymnasium*. After the meeting my classroom teacher told me I should not have made the remark about wanting to become a rector, since it showed lack of modesty. Girls were brought up differently then. Today, having been Director of the University of Pittsburgh's English Language Institute since 1970, I think I wasn't far off the mark. True, the language is English instead of Swedish, but the fascination with language and the joy of teaching have remained the same.

This book is a collection of articles from my writings over the years on teaching English. Except for the introductory encyclopaedia article, the chapters are arranged in chronological order. They all share some basic features. The primary influence on my thinking about language learning and teaching is the empirically observed problems and difficulties students experience in learning a second language, and the articles all reflect this concern. Theoretical speculations are interesting but they serve a very minor part of this volume.

The overriding criterion in selecting these particular articles is that I still agree with the content. Theoretical notions have come and gone, but I still find the basic classroom concerns and procedures that I discuss here as valid as the day I wrote them. Of course proponents of the Natural Way and Suggestopedia will disagree — that is as it should be. Rather, I am saying that within my experience, the points I made in these articles remain valid.

The introductory article 'English Teaching as a Foreign or Second Language' is from the International Encyclopedia of Education. It is not at all controversial and simply serves as an introduction.

'On Creativity and Teaching' is a much abbreviated form of a term paper I wrote for a course at Columbia University. The instructor's comments said something to the effect that I should be more careful in my scholarship. The article remains one of my favorites.

v

During my first year at Pitt, my students, who were teaching assistants in the ELI, asked me to teach a methods course. In a very real sense, 'Sequencing' is a result of that course. Then as now, I think grammar, however you choose to define it, is at the heart of adult second language learning. Then as now, ESL instructors tended to be at the mercy of their textbooks. Ours were classically audio-lingual and much disliked by the instructors (we used the Lado-Fries series and in retrospect it is remarkable that they worked at all).

This article was one of the first attempts to work communication into classroom procedures in an orderly and systematic fashion. Any theoretical linguistic and psycholinguistic remarks need to be taken with caution. But the basic M-M-C sequence of classroom activities (not necessarily in the form of drills) still holds valid in my opinion — an opinion which is shared by others.

The ultimate goal in my teacher-training methods courses has always been the same: to enable teachers to consider and analyse their own teaching dispassionately and objectively. 'The Use of Video-tape' was an effort towards making the point.

Teaching English as a second language often involves teachers and students from different cultures with resultant opportunities for mis-understandings. 'Teaching the Culturally Different Pupil' was written for American public school teachers and lays out some basic concepts for cross-cultural communication. 'Linguistic Interaction' was written for Chinese teachers at the tertiary level and is more concerned with course content, but both articles deal with understanding someone from another culture. These articles, and the two that follow, reflect my continuous interest in anthropology.

'Linguistic and Communicative Competence' was written in Sweden during a sabbatical leave when I worked with people from the British Council who influenced me with their growing concern for communication in teaching. This is a good place to acknowledge the debt I owe them. 'Developing Communicative Competence' is an attempt to implement Dell Hymes' concept of communicative competence for the ESL classroom. I delivered that paper for that first time at Lackland Airforce base in 1974. I was on stage with twelve of the Defence Language Institute students with whom I demonstrated the techniques I advocated. I was too naïve to think it remarkable, but I was told repeatedly afterwards by DLO staff that they would never have believed a word I had said, if they had not seen it with their own eyes. These were new thoughts in 1974.

I have done a fair share of textbook writing in ESL and wanted something to reflect that interest; the two 'Comments' selections do just that. Mostly they are just common sense remarks.

The 'Applied Linguistics' article may be like the old Punch cartoon of the London zookeeper who responded to the old lady's query as to the sex of the hippopotamus by saying that it ought to be of interest only to another hippopotamus. I had been asked to write an article on this topic, thought it boring but went ahead with it, and surprised myself with the findings. I include the article because it has implications for teacher training courses and also suggests reading topics for those who want to study on their own.

There are fashions and bandwagons in TESOL and 'Communicative Competence: Second Thoughts' reflects, and reflects on, those tendencies. Although I don't discuss it in the article, today I think it also reflects the steady growth over the last decades of English as a global language. Talking about communicative competence and global English will have to be done in terms of world Englishes. I touch on that topic in 'Linguistic Interaction' as well. It is a matter which won't go away until the world sees a new lingua franca, but that will never occur in our lifetime.

The last article, 'ESL in Bilingual Education' brings together two consuming interests of mine. It is based on empirical data from many classrooms but raises as many questions as it answers. I find this a suitable article with which to end the book, acknowledging that we don't have all the answers. Once, when Frank Lloyd Wright was asked which he thought was his best house, his answer was 'The next one, always the next one!' It is much the same with scholarship.

Introduction: English — Teaching as a Foreign or Second Language

English as a foreign language (EFL) is concerned with the teaching of English to speakers of other languages (TESOL). Sometimes the reference is to English as a second language (ESL), and this article attempts first to clarify the various acronyms of the field and their reference. The article continues with a discussion of the various domains of TESOL and closes with a brief look at the major trends in the field.

EFL, ESL, and TESOL

The original term for teaching English to those who did not know it and for the area of expertise associated with it, was English as a foreign language, known for short as EFL. On the whole, this continues to be the British usage in referring to overseas teaching of English. In the United States, the term ESL, English as a second language, became increasingly used, and today there are no less than three definitions of the term. American publishers increasingly avoided the term EFL in favor of ESL as they considered the term 'foreign' to be pejorative and so to be avoided in the selling of textbooks. This usage is simply synonymous with EFL and begs the question of any difference between the two. The second usage of ESL refers to the learning of English in an English-speaking environment, such as by foreign students in England or in the United States. Finally, the third usage of ESL defines a second language as the nonhome but official language of a nation which must be learned by its citizens for full social, economic, and political participation in the life of that nation. Australian Aborigines, United States Chicanos, and British Gaelic speakers as well as immigrants all learn English as a second language according to this definition. All three usages are common, but the third is to be preferred because it is the relationship between the super- and subordinate groups within a nation which gives

second language learning its significant characteristics and which distinguishes it from learning a foreign language where attitudes are fairly neutral.

Exactly in order to avoid the dichotomy, EFL and ESL became united
in TESOL, teaching English to speakers of other languages, which stands
both for the field and for the international professional organization, which
was founded in 1966. Unless a technical differentiation is intended, TESOL
is the better cover term for the field.

The Domains of TESOL

The teaching of English to speakers of other languages, as a professional field, is a relative newcomer to language teaching compared to the
teaching of Greek and Latin. Similar to those languages, the spread of
English has also reflected social conditions such as emigration, colonialism,
military power, and trade as well as advanced scientific knowledge, and in
the case of English, advanced technology. The result necessarily has been a
many-faceted picture of English teaching around the world.

Basically the field can be subdivided into four areas: EFL, ESL, bilingual education and ESOD (English to speakers of other dialects) (Robinett,
1972).

EFL (English as a Foreign Language)

The study of English began primarily as learning English as a cultural
acquisition which would enable the learner to read the classics like Shakespeare and Milton in the original. The purpose, objectives, and methods of
this type of English study are very similar to the study of French, German
and Italian as foreign languages.

Today, however, straight EFL overlaps with, and is superseded by,
English as an LWC (language of wider communication), as the major lingua
franca of the world. Until the First World War, French had been the major
language of wider communication within Europe, but after the Second
World War this role has been taken over worldwide by English. This fact
is reflected in the considerable investment in English teaching — in curriculum, textbooks, and teacher training — held by Third World countries
where English is not seen primarily as a cultural acquisition nor as a colonial
legacy but practically as an instrumental means of international communication in an electronic world. It is also reflected in the popularity of the adult
English classes sponsored by the British Council and the United States Bi-
national Centers around the world. The Regional English Language Centre
(RELC) in Singapore is another case in point.

As far as language attitudes are concerned, the study of EFL is the most neutral of the field. There are no external social, religious, or political pressures which enforce the study of English but rather it is a voluntary choice for instrumental or integrative purposes.

ESL (English as a Second Language)

In many parts of the world the study of English takes place because English is an official (or critically important public) language of that nation. This situation is almost always the result of earlier annexation or colonization. Actually, the situations vary widely from countries which are commonly thought of as monolingually English, such as Australia and the United States, to countries which are notedly multilingual such as Nigeria and India.

The purposes and motivations for maintaining English as the official language vary as the situation's social, economic, religious, and political factors vary. In Nigeria, for example, it has served both to neutralize ethnic group interests as well as to promote Pan-Africanism, and so a former colonial language remains tolerated as the official language among several national languages. In India, English remains preferred by many as the national language to the alternative of Hindi with its strong associations to a specific religious sect. In Singapore, English is a practical means of a multiethnic population for carrying on trade with the West. In the United States, English became unofficially (there exists no federal legislation on the matter) the official language for primarily practical concerns, until monolingualism became the idealized norm, although 16.3% of the population report a non-English mother tongue (Waggoner, 1981). The United States is one of the few countries outside Britain in which nationalism has been an issue in English teaching.

The situations vary widely, and so do the attitudes toward the study of English that accompany them. All ESL situations share, by definition, an imposition of English on the learner and often this is perceived as a derogatory comment on the home culture with concomitant social strife. Spanish-speaking Puerto Rico (USA) is a good example of such tension. On the other hand, predominantly Spanish-speaking Gibraltar gladly welcomes English. The reasons for the various attitudes towards and the relative efficiency of learning ESL are ultimately to be found in the social settings (Saville-Troike, 1976).

Bilingual education

The domain of bilingual education within the field of TESOL refers to programs where equal emphasis is placed on learning the native language as well as English. Typically, the literature and discussions of bilingual education do not include elitist schooling which adds a component of EFL to the curriculum of private schools, but rather tend to include the concerns of minority-group children in public schooling where English is taught as a second language. An exception are the Canadian immersion programs where Anglophone children study in French and English, but another defining characteristic of bilingual education holds: the children study subject matter, such as history, through the medium of French, the target language.

Considerable conflict exists over the goals of bilingual education. In the United States, for example, the programs officially are denoted as transitional bilingual education and seen as a more efficient way of teaching the national language where the tacit goals are language shift through bilingualism and assimilation into mainstream culture. (Alaska is an exception.) Many Chicanos, Indians, and Puerto Ricans resent these goals and prefer to maintain their cultural identity of which language is an integral part. Their social goal is cultural pluralism with structural incorporation, that is, access to goods and services and to social institutions like education and justice. The goals of bilingual education, as they see it, are maintenance bilingual education programs, where the programs teach not only the native language but also the native culture. Bilingual programs in which the children speak the national language and which are voluntary tend to avoid such strife.

There is very little systematic knowledge of techniques and procedures for teaching children a second language at the elementary level which is coherently anchored in a theory of language acquisition. The elaboration of such a body of knowledge is an important priority for the future development of bilingual education (Paulston 1980).

English to speakers of other dialects

The last domain of TESOL refers to ESOD (English to speakers of other dialects) or more commonly known as SESD (standard English as a second dialect). Standard English as a second dialect deals with teaching English to those whose home language is a distinct English dialect which differs markedly from standard English, such as the Maoris in New Zealand, the Native Americans in Alaska and Canada, Afro-Americans in the United States, creole speakers in the Caribbean, and so on. Even though the social settings differ widely, the educational problems remain markedly similar.

Since the early 1970s, Caribbean Creoles and Black English have been the focus of intense scholarly interest and work which are reflected in the teaching of standard English (Alleyne, 1980). There were originally attempts to adopt foreign language teaching techniques, but such methods have not turned out very well, and most scholars believe with Allen (1969) that 'A second dialect is not a foreign language'. Some major issues have been: (a) applying linguistic descriptions to studies of interference in reading and writing and consequent implications for teaching; (b) teaching the legitimacy of the dialects as a linguistic system in its own right; (c) the identification of culture-specific speech acts and the legitimacy of the culture itself; (d) language attitudes; and (e) Labov's (1968) *The Study of Non-standard English*.

Altogether, the domains of TESOL range over a wide variety of situations and needs. The particular situation of the learner needs always to be taken into account because the social, political, cultural and economic factors tend to be of far more significance in influencing educational results than any language teaching methods *per se*.

Recent Trends

Foreign language teaching turns primarily to psychology for theory, models, and explanatory frameworks. With the recent concentration on student learning rather than on teaching, cognitive psychology has succeeded behavioral psychology as a more viable approach. Neurolinguistics is an area of study which has recently received much attention, but at this point it is premature to make any direct application to language teaching. In psycholinguistics, the amount of so-called second language acquisition research attests to the increasing emphasis and importance of empirical and quantificational research in language teaching.

In general, language teaching remains eclectic in its methods (Paulston & Bruder, 1976; Rivers & Temperley, 1978; Robinett, 1978). The audio-lingual method has been discredited but no one method has taken its place. Instead there is a plethora of methods among which may be mentioned community counseling–learning, notional–functional syllabi, rapid acquisition, the silent way, suggestopedia, and total physical response. These methods vary widely, and each has its supporters as well as detractors. Actually, as long as teachers and students have confidence that they are in fact learning, and all are happy in the process, methods probably do not make too much difference. Probably the most widespread method in TESOL in spite of all the scholarly criticism remains the grammar-translation approach, but the social incentives are so strong that students learn in spite of the methods.

By far the most important development in TESOL has been the emphasis on a communicative approach in language teaching (Coste, 1976; Roulet, 1972; Widdowson, 1978). The one thing that everyone is certain about is the necessity to use language for communicative purposes in the classroom. Consequently, the concern for teaching linguistic competence has widened to include communicative competence, the socially appropriate use of language, and the methods reflect this shift from form to function.

One more development in TESOL deserves mention, namely the publication of *A Grammar of Contemporary English* (Quirk *et al.*, 1972) and its shorter version *A Concise Grammar of Contemporary English* by Quirk & Greenbaum (1973). As reference grammars, they are not intended for EFL/ESL students, but they nevertheless provide a wealth of information for the English textbook writer, teacher, and serious student alike.

References

ALLEN, V. F. 1969, A second dialect is not a foreign language. In J. ALATIS (ed.) *Linguistics and the Teaching of Standard English to Speakers of Other Languages or Dialects.* Washington, DC: Georgetown University Press.

ALLEYNE, M. 1980, *Comparative Afro-American: An Historical-Comparative Study of English-Based Afro-American Dialects of the New World.* Ann Arbor, Michigan: Karoma.

COSTE, D. 1976, *Un Niveau seuil: Systèmes d'apprentissage des langues vivantes par les adultes.* Strasbourg: Council of Europe.

LABOV, W. 1968, *The Study of the Non-standard English of Negro and Puerto Rican Speakers in New York City.* Washington, DC: ERIC, Center for Applied Linguistics.

PAULSTON, C. B. 1980, *Bilingual Education: Theories and Issues.* Rowley, Massachusetts: Newbury House.

PAULSTON, C. B. and BRUDER, M. N. 1976, *Teaching English as a Second Language: Techniques and Procedures.* Cambridge, Massachusetts: Winthrop.

QUIRK, R. and GREENBAUM, S. 1973, *A Concise Grammar of Contemporary English.* New York: Harcourt Brace Jovanovich.

QUIRK, R., GREENBAUM, S., LEECH, G. and SVARTVIK, J. 1972, *A Grammar of Contemporary English.* New York: Harcourt Brace Jovanovich.

RIVERS, W. M. and TEMPERLEY, M. S. 1978, *A Practical Guide to the Teaching of English as a Second or Foreign Language.* Oxford: Oxford University Press.

ROBINETT, B. W. 1972, The domains of TESOL. *TESOL Quarterly* 6, 197–207.

—— 1978, *Teaching English to Speakers of Other Languges: Substance and Technique.* New York: McGraw-Hill.

ROULET, E. 1972, *Théories grammaticales, descriptions et enseignement des langues.* Nathan, Paris (1975 Linguistic Theory, Linguistic Description and Language Teaching. London: Longman).

SAVILLE-TROIKE, M. 1976, *Foundations for Teaching English as a Second Language: Theory and Method for Multicultural Education.* Englewood Cliffs, NJ: Prentice-Hall.

WAGGONER, D. 1981, Statistics on language use. In C. F. FERGUSON and S. B. HEATH, (eds) *Language in the USA.* Cambridge, Massachusetts: Cambridge University Press.

WIDDOWSON, H. G. 1978, *Teaching Language as Communication.* Oxford: Oxford University Press.

1 On Creativity and Teaching

It was when I was teaching in the American School of Tangier that I first became interested in problems of creativity and the classroom. I certainly did not recognize the problem as such in the beginning: the varied responses in learning behavior I put down to differences in national background. Among the four nationalities represented at the school (Moroccan, Spanish, Indian, and American) my American students were so much like those students I had taught in Minnesota for five years that they did not make much impression on me in the beginning; I merely took them for granted. But then it dawned on me that these students were consistently the best in the class. They placed high on the tests; they frequently did extra work outside of class, and they did not hesitate to question that which they disagreed with or did not understand. Their independence of mind constantly impressed me. For one who had for so long berated American secondary education from the Olympic heights of the European *gymnasium-lycée* traditions, this was quite an acknowledgment, and I began to question and compare.

Educators often overlook significant facts in their teaching situations because they are environmental and, as such, not always noticeable, especially to products of the same environment. It is when we contrast our own environment to another that some things become noticeable; so I shall discuss the experiences which brought me to these thoughts upon creativity and teaching.

Passion and Industry

The Moroccans, and this was my sustained impression (although there were, of course, exceptions), were quite wild. They had, as Jerome Bruner would say, all the passion but no decorum. I still have not reconciled this with the fact that they came from a culture which has traditionally revered learning and which produced the great Karaouine University when European thought was still in its infancy; it may be that the American system allowed these unencumbered spirits too much freedom. It may also be that their authoritarian culture did not foster a sense of self-discipline: although

1

capable of brilliant flashes, they lacked staying power. The facts were that many of the Moroccan students had been in the same school since first grade, being taught exactly what the American students were taught; but there was a marked difference between the two. The Indian students, who came from the large merchant class in Tangier and Gibraltar, were quiet, docile and conscientious. At this point I had them comfortably pegged and had settled down to tame the Moroccans and get some life into the Indians, a procedure which went on in a sporting fashion throughout the year, with the Moroccans ingeniously thinking up new rules for the game.

But halfway through the term I got two new students, Spanish transfers from the local *lycée*. These students would have been a delight to any teacher; they were hard-working, conscientious, neat, and exceedingly polite. It took some time until I discovered that they were incapable of thinking. They would know their lessons by heart; but, when they were asked for an individual judgment, a synthesis, an unorthodox reply, they would become mute. This became so much the pattern for all the later *lycée*-transfers, it became clear that this typical classroom behavior could not merely be ascribed to a different cultural background. The *lycée* pattern of industrious, fact-knowledgeable, and un-thinking students cut across all nationalities, and I was forced to question the very institution which I had always venerated as the epitome of excellence in secondary education. I was bored with these students; there was rarely any excitement in the learning; for them it was a duty to fulfill in order to gain deserved praise. My Moroccans, who were likely to have conniption fits of excitement, were certainly never boring, however fatiguing. As the time went on, and my transfer students were pressured into what I am sure they secretly considered highly unorthodox behavior, their minds loosened up as well as their manners. It seemed to me that an ease of manner always preceded the slow recuperation of thought; and, after about a year, they merged well with the Americans. All of them told me at one time or another that for the first time they understood what they had learned, they enjoyed what they had learned, and that school had been fun. That school could be fun, I think, never did cease to amaze them. The Spanish students probably most clearly exhibited this general trend of behavioral change.

Rewarding Nonconformity

These last years' experience was at the back of my mind when I found myself again in a Swedish *gymnasium*, but this time as the teacher. The students were all highly selected as far as academic ability was concerned, emotionally very mature, and with a great ease of verbal expression. Along with other classes, I taught a course of Swedish literature to a class of young men who, it developed, were virtually incapable of understanding a poem. They were excellent at historical and literary trends, at specific figures of speech and literary forms, and at such matters as could be memorized; but, when asked for the meaning of a specific poem, they would come to a silent halt.

We studied a poet named Kellgren, much beloved by Swedish teachers because he changed schools in midstream and went from a sober classicism to a flaming romanticism. Here is stuff to teach: nice tangible literary trends exemplified in similes, synecdoches, and marching feet. Swedish though I am, I find him dreadful and settled for a discussion of whether he was least dreadful as a classicist or as a romanticist. The class did not approve of such an approach. They considered it a waste of time discussing the poems when they should have been memorizing the facts about the poems; but one very brilliant boy volunteered that surely Kellgren was greater as a romantic poet. I disagreed and challenged his opinion until the boy in exasperation exclaimed, 'But *fröken,* the textbook says so'. I calmly suggested that the textbook might be wrong. In the carefully ordered hierarchy of authority that is a Swedish school, I had challenged the very foundation of their scholastic life, and I had indeed a very nervous class in front of me. The next step was, it seems to me, logical so I proceeded to assure them that I could also perfectly well be wrong and that they ought to trust their own opinions before they accepted mine or the textbook's. This simply had never occurred to them. Time went on. It was a strange teaching experience, where conformity brought scoldings, and disagreements the highest praise. At length my unwilling readers of poetry became more adept, and we could at least settle down to some interesting discussions, even if they never did learn to enjoy poetry.

To enjoy poetry you need to be unafraid, and it was exactly my Swedish students' ready acceptance of authority and all that had led to it that resulted in their not understanding poetry, just as the *lycée*-students had been incapable of independent reasoning for the same kind of reason. This brings us directly to the question of creativity in the classroom. It seems to me that that which represents an obstacle for a creative mind is also an obstacle to meaningful learning.

Creativity and Meaning

It is futile to discuss the significance of creativity. Creativity is no more meaningful than life is meaningful; the meaning lies in the living, and without creativity there is that much less life. We are concerned with creativity, then, as it helps us lead a richer life. As teachers, we are also concerned because it is not possible to understand the manifest creativity of genius — an awkward way to say the great works of art — if one does not have a fair amount of unbound creative spirit within oneself to recognize and become transformed by the greater insight. It is of course essential that the teacher of art, music or literature himself can understand the importance of that which he intends to teach; it is as essential that the students be taught so that they can see the meaning of the creative act and the significance of it to their own lives and not be fogged by fear in the manner of my Swedish students.

We can now turn to consider what we mean by creativity, Sylvia Ashton-Warner, the most creative teacher I knew, sees creativity and destruction as the white and the black angel fighting for the outlet of the child's energy and love as the force that will sway the victory to the white angel. Basically I think that expresses it.

Erich Fromm distinguishes between the creative act and the creative attitude; Abraham Maslow, between 'special talent creativeness' and 'self-actualizing creativeness'. There is a wealth of terminology, but we can distinguish between the creativity of the genius and the creative attitude. The creative attitude is an inborn personality trait in all people. In our culture we see it perhaps most clearly exhibited in children — and slowly disappear in the grown-up through society's pressure for conformity. It is with the creative attitude I as a teacher am concerned, because it is something which can be developed and encouraged and, just as important, discouraged, while the creativity of genius is God-given, which is merely a traditional way of saying that it is conditioned by talent or, if one prefers, by genes.

Creative Attitudes

I see the creative attitude as an ability to perceive freely, to see freshly, to hear, to *feel* the connectedness of the various aspects of the world without and within — a feeling unhampered by cultural preconceptions. I see the creative attitude as an ability to see and to respond to the significance of life as it strikes us — always new and marvelous. This seems a very simple thing, yet it is not. The anthropologists are constantly showing us how conditioned we are by the specific cultures into which we happen to be born and how incapable we are of seeing the world unhampered by our specific language and culture. Dorothy Lee (1959) convincingly points out that our dependence on linear reasoning has made us incapable of any other as well as unable to think of our existence in any other terms than those of causality and modality. I suspect that our creative attitude or our creative inner life is not linear, and from this arises one of the difficulties of coming to terms with it.

It is difficult here to avoid a discussion of reality and truth. Philosophers make the useful and, I think, essential differentiation between literal truth and artistic truth. Literal truth belongs to our physical world, to the laboratories and their experiments, while artistic truth belongs to the realms of inner life. I am not sure that it is necessary to consider which of the two is more significant to our lives; I myself believe that it is the latter. A dichotomy between the two results in either a compulsive-obsessive neurosis if we believe in nothing but literal fact, or in schizophrenia if literal facts cease to have importance.

Niall's Bull

It is interesting to consider children's perception in this matter of 'reality'. Four-year-old Niall's drawing of a bull, shown in Figure 1.1, shows the bull with a multitude of horns; the *literal* fact is that a bull has but two horns which I imagine Niall can see as well as I. The *artistic* fact is that the bull's physical strength and masculine power, which after all is the significant truth about a bull, is symbolically expressed in his horns, and through a bit of redundancy Niall merely emphasized this aspect of the bull. It may be relevant to consider that the bull has from times immemorial been a powerful participant in religious ritual — from Crete's bulldancers to today's bullfights and sacred cows — and has always inspired powerful symbolism. It is quite true that I never, although I literally knew about bulls and rituals and sexual symbols, would see a bull with many horns. Niall's perception is much fresher and closer to artistic truth than is my literal and impoverished eye.

What have I lost then that I cannot see a bull with many horns, that I cannot immediately perceive the basic significance of a thing that a four-year-old understands instinctively with no need to rationalize? Surely it is a limitation of my creative ability. I believe strongly that one reason for this loss is what Marshall McLuhan calls our society's obsession with data classification and the lack of emphasis on the importance of pattern recognition. Our entire educational system is concerned with data classification, and I suggest that this delimits the creative ability of perception because it is based on the visual sense to the exclusion of the others, and this results in a skewed balance and in an inability to perceive completely. Data classification cannot deal with artistic truth, since its medium is a discursive one. Pattern recognition, on the other hand (and teaching by concepts is one aspect of it), is as easily at home with discursive as with presentational symbols and so does not

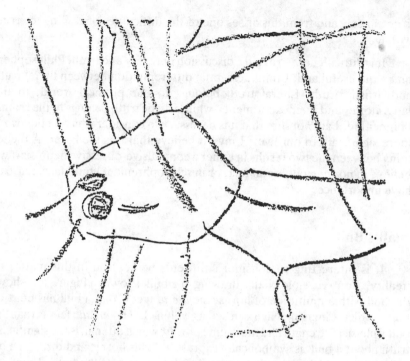

FIGURE 1.1   *The Bull — drawing by Niall Johnson, 4*

hinder the perception of artistic truth, which should not be thought of as diametrically opposed to literal truth; it is merely another aspect of our perception of reality, and we certainly need both in order to live a full life. 'A bull has two horns' is data classification. 'A bull has fourteen horns' is also data classification, although false. The creative expression is non-verbal, non-discursive, and the meaning of Niall's drawing lies within the drawing.

Creative Energies

The other and main reason for the, I am sure, substantial loss of my creative ability, of my powers of complete perception and response to the world beyond and within, is a partial damming or blocking of the sources of creativity. It is very difficult to talk about this as there is not yet a very good vocabulary for it but, since Freud was the pioneer in new understanding, his terms are frequently used. I see creativity as a form of energy of the psyche released when there is a healthy relationship between the conscious and the unconscious. This energy, the source of creativity, grows with use and will contribute to the health of the psyche, just as the healthy psyche releases energy for creative activity. (As I have said, the psyche does not gracefully lend itself to linear reasoning.) I think it basic that teachers understand this. Especially as a teacher of teenagers, one is at times amazed by the complete self-preoccupation of one's students. Their psychic energy is diverted from the creative outlets of relationship in being occupied with the inner conflicts of puberty. It is much easier to deal with and understand teenagers if one thinks of them as mildly and temporarily insane, and to the degree that the diverted psychic energy is a sign of something less than 'the whole man' they are. I have, at times, in exasperation suggested this to my high school students, and it has always struck them as a delightful and eminently sound observation.

It was exactly this creative energy my Swedish students lacked and which made it difficult for them to perceive the specific kind of symbolism which is poetry. I have earlier suggested as causes their fear and dependency on authority. These may seem completely unrelated, but it is merely another way of saying that their psychic energy was delimited because of the domination of their consciousness by a strong superego.

The authoritarian system reinforces the superego through fear and anxiety; the psyche is then preoccupied with the uneven balance of the conscious and unconscious. In its turn, the superego reinforces and depends on authority to justify its existence. It will shy away from that which will threaten its precarious rule, shy from understanding free-flying insights into the mysterious life of the psyche which all art is, from making independent judgments of poetry to history and chemistry. The insecure psyche will not move without the assurance of authority, and so my *lycée* students could not think — to think freely and independently is another aspect of the creative attitude.

The Fat King

I have noted in myself that it is only the last years that I have become capable of reading certain types of poetry.

Remembering in Oslo the old Picture of the Magna Carta

The girl in the house dress, pushing open the window,
Is also the fat king sitting under the oak tree,
And the garbage men, thumping their cans, are

Crows still cawing,
And the nobles are offering the sheet to the king.
One thing is also another thing, and the doomed galleons,
Hung with trinkets, hove by the coast, and in the blossoms
of trees are still sailing on their long voyage from Spain;
I too am still shocking grain, as I did as a boy, dog tired,
And my great-grandfather steps on his ship. (Bly, 1962: 30)

How can the girl be a fat king? Who is the king? Garbage men! But this
is data classification, and even if we know that the king is King John of
England (1199–1216), it tells us nothing about the poem. The superego-
dominated mind prefers to deal with literal fact, it wants to be provedly correct and praised by authority, and it is fear that hampers the understanding
of a poem. I am not so sure that we have a word for the un-fear that we need
but certainly love is its basic part. The source of love as well as of the creative
attitude is the psychic energy we have spoken about. It takes un-fear, the
security which comes with love, not to worry about the meaning of this
poem. It is understandable that an English teacher, who will have to teach
the poem, will worry about the meaning, and that may be one reason that
most teaching of poetry falls in the data classification category. It takes love
to see that a simple girl is the same thing as a king; it takes love to encompass
the sameness of man's experience and the strangeness of it which is one thing
the poem is about. It also takes un-fear to admit that I still don't understand
this poem and not to be worried about it and still to read it and find it meaningful.

And this brings us to symbols and the metaphoric mode of knowing.
Susanne Langer distinguishes between discursive and presentational symbols. Language is in itself a symbol; the meaning of *cat* lies not in the sound
of /kaet/ but in the thing for which it stands. Language has units which lend
themselves to lexical treatment and can be defined as well as it also has a
system for organizing these units which system can be described exactly. So
have the symbols for mathematics and chemistry. They are discursive symbols. But, says Langer, 'The limits of language are not the last limits of
experience, and things inaccessible to language may have their own forms of
conception, that is to say, their own symbolic devices' (Langer, 1964: 237).
These are the presentational or non-discursive symbols of art, of the dance,
of music and of poetry, which have no definable units or systems of organization. Langer continues: 'In a general way literal meaning belongs to words
and artistic meaning to images invoked by words and to presentational symbols'. Artistic truth, then, as the revelation of the inner life, as an insight into
human passion, deals with Wittgenstein's 'the unspeakable' and cannot use
discursive language to communicate but does so through its own language,

which is presentational symbols. This explains the at times maddening refusal of the artist or poet to explain or discuss his creation; he simply cannot do so in words. The explanation of his insight lies in his use of presentational symbols: the explanation is in the work of art.

I like to think of presentational symbols as the language of discussion between the conscious and the unconscious, and in order to follow this discussion we need creative energy. The main manifestations of this discussion we find in our dreams, in all forms of art, and in ritual and religion. We are to a much greater degree than we normally think of surrounded by ritual which is the attempt to formally externalize the inner conflicts of the individual within the society. James Wright expresses much more significantly what I have been trying to say about ritual, fear, love, and the inner life of man:

Autumn Begins in Martins Ferry, Ohio

In the Shreve High football stadium,
I think of Polacks nursing long beers in Tiltonsville,
And gray faces of Negroes in the blast furnace at Benwood.

And the ruptured night watchman of Wheeling Steel,
Dreaming of heroes.

All the proud fathers are ashamed to go home.
Their women cluck like starved pullets,
Dying for love.

Therefore,
Their sons grow suicidally beautiful
At the beginning of October,
And gallop terribly against each other's bodies. (Wright, 1963: 15)

References

BLY, R. 1962, *Silence in the Snowy Fields*. Middletown, Conn.: Wesleyan University Press.
LANGER, S. K. 1964, *Philosophy in a New Way*. New York: New American Library.
LEE, D. 1959, *Freedom and Culture*. Englewood Cliffs, NJ: Prentice Hall.
WRIGHT, J. 1963, *The Branch Will Not Break*. Middletown, Conn.: Wesleyan University Press.

2 The Sequencing of Structural Pattern Drills

Prescript. The original article, published in 1971, was one of the earlier calls for communicative elements in language teaching. I have here deleted the majority of the references to the literature as they are now very dated, but have left a few as I find them historically interesting. And I still believe, as I did then, that there are likely to be aspects of memorization and habit-formation in adult foreign language learning, whatever present fads expound.

This paper is a discussion of drills, now much in disfavor, but the basic principles apply to most form focused classroom activities.

There is at present in the field of language learning and teaching a reexamination of many of its basic tenets and assumptions. This paper is an attempt to reexamine the role and function of structural pattern drills in language learning. The first part of the paper seeks to examine the relevant literature pertaining to drills in order to (1) bring together some of the major references for comparison of agreements and disagreements and (2) to consider the implications for language teaching. The second part of the paper proposes a theoretical classification of structural pattern drills, incorporating the implications found relevant, in order to provide a systematic and more efficient working model for the classroom.

A cursory glance at the literature during the last two decades reveals a consistent concern about drills, their function, construction, and role in language teaching. This concern naturally reflects the assumptions about language learning held by the advocates of the present major approach to teaching foreign languages, the audio-lingual method. Language learning is seen as basically a mechanical system of habit formation, strengthened by reinforcement of the correct response; language is verbal, primarily oral, behavior and as such learned only by inducing the students to 'behave'. (See Rivers, 1964, Summary of Table of Content, vii–viii.) It is not by accident that most of the proponents of this method are or are trained by descriptive structural linguists, since, as Croft points out, pattern practice and substitution drills — the very backbone of the original Fries' oral method — developed from techniques of linguistic field methods (Croft, 1965: 45). It is interesting to speculate that part of the theoretical foundations of the audio-lingual method was based on a fortuitous, albeit very felicitous, fit between the then major linguistic method of analysis and psychological learning theory.

Scientists tend to do research on what they have the instruments to investigate, and linguists are no exception. Surely there is a relationship between kinds of linguistic analyses and kinds of drills, in that drills attempt to teach what linguistic analysis reveals of language structure and typically, different linguistic analyses explore different characteristics of language structure. So Moulton as early as 1963 pointed out the relationship between tagmemics and substitution drills, between immediate constituent grammar and expansion drills and between transformation-generative theory and transformation drills (Moulton, 1963: 11–15). I think this is important to consider in light of the present challenge of the basic tenets of the audio-lingual method.

> Linguists have had their share in perpetuating the myth that linguistic behavior is 'habitual' and that a fixed stock of 'patterns' is acquired through practice and used as the basis for analogy. These views could be maintained only as long as grammatical description was sufficiently vague and imprecise. (Chomsky, 1966: 44)

There has been relatively little disagreement on the purpose of structural pattern drills when one looks at the literature of the past 20 years. Drills

> are undertaken solely for the sake of practice, in order that performance may become habitual and automatic, [and] make no pretense of being communication. (Brooks, 1964: 146)

> The function of drill is to provide sufficient repetition in meaningful context to establish correct habitual responses. (Bowen, 1965: 295)

> The fact that language operates largely on the basis of habit should be obvious to everyone . . . what is needed is practice that will gradually force the students' attention away from the linguistic problem while forcing them to use language examples that contain the problem. This will engage the habit mechanism and more quickly establish the new habits. (Lado, 1964: 105)

Linguists from Fries (1945: 8–9) to Haugen (1959) to Moulton (1963: 5) have echoed the belief that language learning is habit formation. Obviously we need now to look very closely at how this is reflected in structural pattern drills. There also seems to be disagreement on the degree of meaning necessary in drills and I shall return to this question.

There is within the last five, six years a definite increase in the demand for some form of meaning and communication in the drills. Wilga Rivers (1968: 82) throughout her *Teaching Foreign Language Skills* emphasizes the need for meaningful learning and communicative classroom activities. Clifford Prator (1967) has a very useful paper where he outlines Bowen's (1965: 292–309), Stevick's (1966) and his own viewpoints on this and their variances, but basically they all agree that there are two poles in language learning, i.e. from manipulation to communication, and that in efficient language teaching there needs to be some form of communication built into the drills. For once, there is experimental evidence to support this assumption. Oller & Obrecht (1968) report on an experiment carried out in a Rochester, New York high school with the conclusion that 'the effectiveness of a given pattern is significantly increased by relating the language of that drill to communicative activity in the teaching/learning process'. They conclude that from the very first stages of foreign language study meaningful communicative activity should be a, if not the, central point of pattern drills.

To sum up, there are fairly adequate procedural descriptions of types of drills available, although we need to consider the implications of recent linguistic theory on new types of drills (not within the scope of this paper). There is growing concern with the necessity to teach not only parroting of the teacher but also some form of communication within the classroom. We do not have as yet a generally accepted theoretical framework for classifying structural pattern drills, which deals with these problems.

I have recently (Paulston, 1970) attempted in an article called 'Structural pattern drills: a classification' to suggest such a conceptual framework; that is, a classification that recognizes that language learning is partly but not only habit formation, which proposes to put meaning and communication into classroom activities, and to do so in a consistent and orderly procedure. This paper is an attempt to further expand and clarify this proposition for classifying drills. We need such a classification for grading and sequencing drills in order to obtain a systematic and more efficient progression in the classroom from mechanical learning to the internalizing of competence. I believe — with John Carroll (1971), Wilga Rivers (1968) and others in our field — that 'there is no reason to believe that the two positions (language teaching as formation of language habits versus the establishment of rule governed behavior) are mutually exclusive' (Rivers, 1968: 78). Rivers points out in a fascinating footnote that many of the language features which are most efficiently taught by drills (person and number inflections, gender agreements, formal features of tense, etc.) 'are excluded by Chomsky from his system of rewrite rules and are included in the lexicon as parts of complex symbols' (Rivers, 1968: 79).

If, as the evidence seems to suggest, language involves more than one level and there are at least two types of learning (Rivers, 1964: 47, 50), then this should be reflected in the nature and types of drills. Language learning can be conceived of as a three-stage process but, as Prator (1967: 31) points out, there is no way of accurately assigning a drill to a specific stage. My contention is that there are three classes of drills: mechanical, meaningful, and communicative and that we may distinguish these three classes from each other if we analyze the drills in terms of (1) expected terminal behavior, (2) degree of response control, (3) the type of learning process involved, and (4) criteria for selection of utterance response.

But before I proceed to a discussion of the criteria for classifying drills, we need to consider an important aspect of drills, which cuts across this classification. Many have recognized a basic division in kinds of drills. Etmekjian (1966: 33–6) refers to them as teaching drills and testing drills, Rivers (1968) as the teaching phase and the testing phase, and Fries (1945: 9) spoke of patterns produced 'on the level of conscious choice'. What is involved is the difference between drills that serve primarily to help the student memorize a pattern with virtually no possibility for mistake and the drills which test or reinforce the learning of that pattern. The concord of person and verb in the Romance languages serves as a good example for a teaching drill:

Model:	andar (tu)	**R:**	andas
	cantar (tu)		cantas

Continue the drill:

Cue:	trabajar (tu)	**R:**
	pasar (tu)	
	hablar (tu)	

This is a memorizing drill, where even the reader who does not know (or understand) Spanish can complete the drill correctly. But as soon as we change the cues to include all persons, that is to change the cues so as to require an answer of more than minimal items, we require that the student know all the verb endings for the ar-verbs, present tense, and by his response we know whether he does or not. The response depends on the conscious choice of the student:

Model: andar (tu)   **R:** andas
             cantar (Vd.)   **R:** canta

Continue the drill:

Cue: trabajar (el)   **R:**

Only the student who has previously memorized these patterns can complete the drill successfully.

I have constructed a tentative design (shown in Figure 2.1) to clarify the overall division of drills. Drills are basically divided into teaching (memorizing, habituation) drills and testing (feedback, quizzing) drills. There are two types of drill to help the student memorize: repetition drills and mechanical$_1$ drills, which basically tend to be substitution drills, but transformation drills are also possible. The testing drills in turn can be divided according to purpose: acquiring mechanical skill through muscle habituation on the one hand, and on the other internalizing of rules through cognitive processes. The mechanical skill drills subdivide into mechanical$_2$ and meaningful drills while the internalizing of competence drills subdivide into communicative drills and actual communication. It can thus be seen that it is possible for mechanical drills to be either testing or teaching drills, depending on their breakdown into minimal items. I mention this before discussion of the three classes — mechanical, meaningful, and communicative — of drills because this duality of mechanical drills troubled me for a long time and contributed to some confusion in my other article.

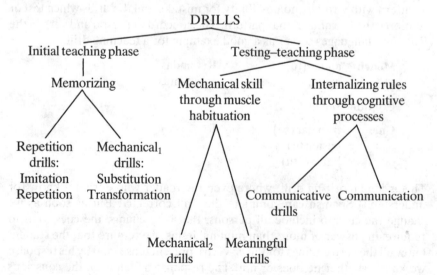

FIGURE 2.1   *Division of drills*

The chart in Table 2.1 may make the following discussion somewhat clearer.

TABLE 2.1   *Classification of drills*

	Mechanical drills	Meaningful drills	Communicative drills
Expected terminal behavior	Automatic use of manipulative patterns — formation of habits	Automatic use of manipulative patterns — formation of habits still working on habit formation	Normal speech for communication — free transfer of patterns to appropriate situations
Degree of control	Complete	Less control but there is a 'right answer' expected	No control of lexical items — some control of patterns. Answer cannot be anticipated
Learning process involved	Learning through instrumental conditioning by immediate reinforcement of correct response ANALOGY	Learning through instrumental conditioning by immediate reinforcement of correct response ANALOGY trial-and-error ANALYSIS	Problem solving ANALYSIS
Criteria for selecting response	Teacher	Teacher, situation, readings (knowledge common to the class)	Student himself (new information about real world)

A mechanical drill is defined as a drill where there is complete control of the response, where there is only one correct way of responding. Because of the *complete* control, the student need not even understand the drill even though he responds correctly, as in the first Spanish drill. One might possibly consider repetition drills as the most extreme example of this class of drill.

Substitution drills lend themselves particularly well to this. Here is another mechanical drill that all readers can complete because it has been broken down to minimal items. It is a memorizing drill on the subject-adjective word order in Thai:

Example:
    +   3   +
    Poom: nakrian Poom

    +   3   +
    suun: nakrian suun

    2   3   2
    ?uan: nakrian ?uan

Continue the drill:

        +
1. naaw

        3
2. roon

3. dii

        2
4. suay

(Anthony *et al.*, 1967: 31)

The following drill is also a mechanical drill but unless you have studied (and memorized) the various classifiers you will not be able to complete it. It is a mechanical testing drill and (apart from the choice of numeral) there is only one correct answer:

6: V 22 Complete the sentence with a numeral and a classifier.

          +   3   3
Example: Kaw suu roon Taaw

         +   3   3   +   2
    Kaw suu roon Taaw soon Kuu

Continue the drill:

    +   3 2 2
1. Kaw suu Paanun

    2   1   3
2. Poo Puuk nekTay

    2   1 2
3. maeae say soyKoo

    3   3 2
4. noon sak sua

        3   1 2 +
8. nakrian say suanaaw

            3   3
9. Kruu suu roonTaaw

         2 3
10. Pii sak kaankeen

        1   2 + 1   +   44
11. dek Puuyin say waeaen

(Anthony *et al.*, 1967: 115)

The difference between a mechanical memorizing drill and a mechanical testing drill lies in the ability of the student to respond, which again depends on how well he has memorized certain patterns, but understanding what he is saying is not a necessary requisite. It is perfectly possible to supply a verb with a correct ending in, e.g. Spanish, without necessarily knowing what the verb means: given Cue: *gratar (nosotros), any docile student will respond with *gratamos and he no more than I will know the meaning of that nonsense word. I remember perfectly well drilling classifiers in Thai without knowing the lexical meaning of the words; I just divided the world in terms of fruits, containers and people, but what kind of people or fruits I did not need to know. The ability to drill mechanical drills without necessarily understanding them is an important criterion in distinguishing them from meaningful drills.

Transformation drills may be mechanical:

John kicked the door.
The door was kicked by John.

All the student need memorize is the structural change and he can complete such a drill without understanding exactly what he is saying. Response drills, which so frequently are being masqueraded forth as communication, can be some of the easiest mechanical drills for the student:

Which would you prefer, tea or coffee?
wine or beer?
nectar or ambrosia?

I know very well that the student is going to answer 'ambrosia' without the foggiest notion of what it is.

The expected terminal behavior of such drills is the automatic use of manipulative patterns and is commensurate with the assumption that language learning is habit formation. It involves the classical Skinnerian method of learning through instrumental conditioning by immediate reinforcement of the right response. Learning takes place through analogy and allows transfer of identical patterns. This is clearly the mechanical level of learning, and this class of drills provides practice in mechanical associations such as adjective-noun agreement, verb-endings, question-forms and the like. This is a very necessary step in language learning, and as long as the student is learning, he won't mind the mechanical nature of the drill. The teacher needs to remember that the student can drill without understanding and to make sure that in fact he does understand. Because of the response-control, it is eminently suited for choral drills.

The student knows how to select his utterance response on the basis of the teacher's cue, be it oral or pictorial, but the teacher is the sole criterion for supplying the correct response. This becomes an important distinction between meaningful and communicative drills.

Much of the criticism of the audio-lingual method is based on the mechanical drill or rather the over-use to which it has been put. There are a number of psychological studies which demonstrate that there is a limit to the efficiency of mechanical drills in the language learning. While not denying the need for mechanical drills, we may note that on the mechanical level alone the student certainly cannot yet express his own ideas fluently. He next needs to work through a set of meaningful drills:

1. **Teacher:** for five years   **Student:** How long did he (study)?
2. **Teacher:** during March   **Student:** When did he (register)?
3. **Teacher:** until four o'clock   **Student:**

In a meaningful drill there is still control of the response although it may be correctly expressed in more than one way and as such less suitable for choral drilling. There is a right answer and the student is supplied with the information necessary for responding, either by the teacher, the classroom situation or the assigned reading, but in all cases the teacher always knows what the student ought to answer. Everyone is always aware that these drills are only language exercises and that any answer will do as well as another as long as it is grammatically correct and conforms to the information supplied. The student cannot complete these drills without fully understanding structurally and semantically what he is saying. I have attempted very hard to exclude lexical meaning from structural in the definition of meaningful drills, but I doubt that it is either possible or desirable. With the new license for mentalism I shall include both. The result is that some pattern drills come very close to being vocabulary drills. Compare the above 'Which would you rather have, tea or coffee?' with 'Which would you rather be, rich and healthy or sick and poor?' In other words, some meaningful drills may have the check for feedback that the student really understands the pattern built into the lexical components.

Comprehension type question and answers based on assigned readings fall in this class of drills:

Teacher: What time did John come to school?
Student: John came to school at 9 o'clock.

as well as much 'situational' teaching as in this drill on post-nominal modification using prepositional phrases, where the students were instructed to describe each other:

Teacher: Which boy is in your class?
Student: The thin boy with long sideburns.
   The handsome boy with black hair.
                                        Etc.

It will be noticed that in the question–answer drill above, the long answers were given. The expected terminal behavior is the same as for mechanical drills. We still want an automatic use of language manipulation; we are still working on habit formation. Although for the language teacher, who is fluent in the target language, it may be difficult to appreciate the enormous difference in difficulty in these two classes of drills.

This is not to deny that a response like 'The man was bitten by the dog', albeit in a mechanical drill, is much more difficult for the learner than a single lexeme substitution drill. Language learning is also the ability to control an increasing amount of language in mechanical manipulation, and we need to consider the difficulty level within the 'amount range' as well.

But the method is different. Mechanical drills by their nature can be drilled without grammatical analysis with the students left to 'analogize' the pattern on their own. This is not possible with meaningful drills. Unless the student understands what he is doing, i.e. recognizes the characteristic features involved in the language manipulation, he cannot complete the drill. Politzer (1968) reports on an interesting experiment in 'The role and place of the explanation in the pattern drill' and points out that an early introduction of the explanation seems to be a more effective treatment than its postponement or omission and that it is preferable to show the application and relevance of the new material in some sort of context before explaining it. The place for the explanation, then, is following the mechanical drills; those students who grasped the analogy will be rewarded with positive reinforcement and those who did not will be helped to understand the specific characteristics of that language structure (Barrutia, 1966). The learning process varies depending on the structural pattern drilled, and while there may still be instrumental conditioning involved, there is very often a trial-and-error process involved in finding the correct response.

At this point, however, there is still no real communication taking place. Students have a tendency to learn what they are taught rather than what we think we are teaching. If we want fluency in expressing their own opinions, then we have to teach that. The expected terminal behavior in communicative drills is normal speech for communication or, if one prefers, the free transfer of learned language patterns to appropriate situations.

The degree of control in a communicative drill is a moot point. I originally stated that there is no control of the response, that the student has free choice to say whatever he wants. However, this turns out not to be true. All classroom teachers, using this system of sequencing drills, have reported back saying that there is indeed control, not of lexical items as we had at first thought but of structural patterns. The difficulty lies just in retaining this control so that the students indeed practice what they have learned; they themselves lose track of the fact that they are drilling and become engrossed in exchanging information. But it is a drill rather than free communication because we are still within the realm of the cue-response pattern. Communication

> requires interpersonal responsiveness, rather than the mere production of language which is truthful, honest, accurate, stylistically pleasing, etc. — those characteristics which look at language as language rather than as behavior, which is the social purpose of language. Our end product is surely getting things done, easing social tensions, goading ourselves into doing this or that, and persuading others to do things. Communication arises when language is used as such interpersonal behaviour, which goes beyond meaningful and truthful manipulation of language symbols. (Johnson, 1970)

To recapitulate, the differences between a meaningful drill and a communicative drill lie in the expected terminal behavior (automatic use of language manipulation versus free transfer of learned language patterns to appropriate situations) and in response control. But the main difference between a meaningful drill and a communicative drill is that in the latter the speaker adds *new* information about the real world. All of us have seen a meaningful drill turn communicative when the students suddenly took the question or cue personally and told us something about himself that we did not know from the classroom situation: 'I have three sisters' is communicative, but 'My shirt is red' is merely meaningful; that information is supplied by the situation, and I can see it as well as the student.

Language teachers have always used communicative drills in the classroom (where else is one asked such personal questions as 'Did you brush your teeth this morning?'), but my point is that there should be an orderly progression from mechanical drilling through meaningful to communicative drills, that the teacher should know one from the other, and that one should not rely on chance that the students will turn a drill into communicative activity.

Communicative drills are the most difficult to arrange within the classroom. They can, of course, never be drilled chorally. Still, if we want fluency in expressing personal opinion, we have to teach that. One way of working with communicative drills is to structure the classroom activity so that it simulates the outside world of the students and to work within this situation. Need I point out that running through a memorized dialogue with accompanying gestures and action is not communicative drill nor necessarily language learning; non-language teachers refer to such activity as acting. Another, simpler way of working with communicative drills is simply to instruct students to answer truthfully.

Example:
1. What is your responsibility?
   My responsibility is   to (learn English).
                                  (learning English).
2. What's your hobby?
   My hobby is   to (make models).
                                  (making models).
3. What's your favorite pastime?
4. What are your lab instructions?
5. What will your occupation be?
6. What are your interests?
7. What is your advice to (Ahmed)?
(Rutherford, 1968: 175)

Gone is the instrumental conditioning; there is no facilitating of the correct response. What we have is John Carroll's (1953: 188)

> 'problem-solving' situation in which the student must find . . . appropriate verbal responses for solving the problem, 'learning' by a trial-and-error process, to communicate rather than merely to utter the speech patterns in the lesson plan.

We are clearly working within a level of language that involves thought and opinion and teaching it in a way that necessitates an understanding of the essential elements of what is being learned. It is a very different experience from mechanical drilling. It is indeed practice in performance by practice in generating new utterances in order to internalize the rules of grammar so that competence will not be defective. I am not saying that language teaching should be concerned solely with communicative type drills, but I am suggesting that any amount of mechanical drills will not lead to competence in a language, i.e. fluency to express one's own opinions in appropriate situations.

To summarize, in language teaching we ought to classify the drills we use into three classes: mechanical, meaningful, and communicative in order to reach free communication. We then need to proceed systematically, not leaving out any one step. Mechanical drills are especially necessary in beginning courses and in learning languages markedly different from the native tongue, such as Thai is for me. I do not believe that this is the only way of teaching languages because it patently is not. Rather, given what we know about languages and learning today, this classification of drills will provide for more efficient language learning.

References

ANTHONY, E. M. *et al.* 1967, *Foundations of Thai — Book 1, Part 1*. Pittsburgh: University of Pittsburgh Press.

BARRUTIA, R. 1966, Some pedagogical dangers in recent linguistic trends. *IRAL* IV, 3, 157–64.

BOWEN, J. D. 1965, Appendix: Pedagogy. In R. P. STOCKWELL, J. D. BOWEN and J. W. MARTIN *The Grammatical Structures of English and Spanish*. Chicago: University of Chicago Press.

BROOKS, N. 1964, *Language and Language Learning*. New York: Harcourt, Brace and World.

CARROLL, J. B. 1953, *The Study of Language*. Cambridge, Mass.: Harvard University Press.

—— 1971, Current issues in psycholinguistics and second language teaching. Paper read at the TESOL convention, New Orleans, March 3–7.

CHOMSKY, N. 1966, Linguistic theory. In R. G. MEAD (ed.) *North East Conference on the Teaching of Foreign Languages*. Report of the working committees.

CROFT, K. 1965, TESL materials development. In K. CROFT (ed.) *NAFSA Studies and Papers* English Language Series, No. 11.

ETMEKJIAN, J. 1966, *Pattern Drills in Language Teaching*. New York: New York University Press.

FRIES, C. C. 1945, *Teaching and Learning English as a Foreign Language*. Ann Arbor: University of Michigan Press.

HAUGEN, E. 1959, *New Paths in American Language Teaching*. ELEC Publications, III, 23.

JOHNSON, F. C. 1970, personal communication from then Professor of English at the University of Papua and New Guinea, now at Kenda University, Japan.

LADO, R. 1964, *Language Teaching: A Scientific Approach*. New York: McGraw-Hill.

MOULTON, W. 1963, What is structural drill? In F. W. GRAVIT and A. VALDMAN (eds) *Structural Drill and the Language Laboratory*. The Hague: Mouton.

OLLER, J. W. and OBRECHT, D. H. 1968, Pattern drill and communicative activity: a psycholinguistic experiment. *IRAL* VI, 2, 165–74.

PAULSTON, C. B. 1970, Structural pattern drills, a classification. *Foreign Language Annals* IV, 2, 187–93.

POLITZER, R. L. 1968, The role and place of the explanation in the pattern drill. *IRAL VI*, 4, 315–31.

PRATOR, C. 1967, Guidelines for planning classes and teaching materials. *Workpapers in English as a Second Language: Matter, Methods, Materials*. Los Angeles: Department of English, University of California.

RIVERS, W. M. 1964, *The Psychologist and the Language Teacher*. Chicago: University of Chicago Press.

—— 1968, *Teaching Foreign Language Skills*. Chicago: University of Chicago Press.

RUTHERFORD, W. E. 1968. *Modern English: A Textbook for Foreign Students*. New York: Harcourt, Brace and World.

STEVICK, E. W. 1966, UHF and microwaves in transmitting language skills. *IJAL* 32, 1, 84–94.

3 The Use of Video-tape in the Training of Foreign Language Teachers

The use of video-tape (VT) in training teachers of foreign languages is a fairly recent development in teacher education. As an alarming amount of this new technique is by necessity carried out on a trial-and-error basis, it might be useful to recount here our experiences with VT during the past year at the University of Pittsburgh. I work primarily with English as a foreign language, but I also have teachers of French and Spanish, and if one thing has become clear, it is that the target language is not a variable that needs consideration. Good language teaching is good language teaching whatever the language, and the procedure in using VT remains the same.

The disadvantages of using VT in teacher training are so obvious and so immediate that all but a very determined instructor will soon give up. There are procedural difficulties of scheduling and coordinating, of breakdown of equipment and of hauling either equipment or students around. VT is exceedingly time consuming if properly used in a methods course, and the preparation of demonstration films even more so. We have just prepared a 40-minute demonstration film for a Spanish teachers' workshop; it took 18 man-hours to prepare it, counting the filming, selection of suitable teaching episodes, and the final editing. VT should not be undertaken as a spur of the moment thing as I did with my first go at it.

Whether the advantages of VT outweigh these initial difficulties depends on one's basic attitude to teacher training. I believe that in teaching skills and techniques, demonstration and practice are as important as theory. (Let it be said somewhere that ultimately teaching is an art. But even Arthur Rubenstein must practice and perfect his techniques. Talent is necessary in all art, but it is not sufficient, and it is the technique aspect we are concerned with here.) VT can serve the demonstration and practice aspects of the methods course[1] in unique ways. A renumeration of the advantages really becomes a list of the various functions of VT.

Basically these functions fall in two categories: VT used (1) for demonstration classes where the language teacher learns to observe and analyze the teaching of others and (2) for practice classes where he learns to analyze his own classroom behavior.

VT is very suitable for demonstration classes of a master teacher in full flight. The tape can be stopped while the class discusses aspects of the teaching, it can be backed and replayed instantly, and it can be edited to contain only those behaviors the instructor wants to discuss.

What most distinguishes it from regular demonstration films available for rental or purchase is that the methods instructor can prepare his own demonstration films to suit his own curriculum. These demonstration films can then be saved and indexed in a reference VT library at small cost.

The demonstration tapes are used in primarily three ways: (1) as 'standard' lessons, (2) for teaching techniques of classroom observation and analysis, and (3) for teaching application of theory to procedures. I use them as demonstration of good teaching as does everyone else, but there is one aspect of this that seems to be overlooked. When we language teachers informally evaluate our own classes, the criterion or standard by which we measure them is usually earlier classes we have taught ourselves for the simple reason that we rarely have access to other teachers' classes, much less an evaluation of them. It is important for the experienced teacher as well as for the novice that he be supplied a collection of standard lessons against which he as a language teacher can compare his own performance, that he observe in practice as well as in theory what good methods in teaching really are. A standard lesson then is a yardstick, a lesson selected by an experienced methods instructor to demonstrate soundness in techniques and procedures.

But it is not enough merely to observe good teaching. It does not follow that the teacher understands what he sees. The second way I use demonstration VTs is as an initial step in learning to analyze classroom behavior, i.e. to isolate the various elements of a class such as presentation of teaching points, different types and classes of drills, explication of grammar by analogy or by analysis, etc. VT is also excellent for teaching various tools of examining classroom behavior, such as the Flanders-Amidon Interaction Analysis. It should be fairly evident that the first step in learning to analyze one's own teaching behavior is to learn the techniques of such analysis and to practice such analysis on others where the learner need not also worry about personal feelings and reactions.

If I said earlier that observation and practice are as important as theory in a methods course, that is not to imply that theory is not important. Without sound theory, no amount of practice will serve because future decisions as to the soundness of innovations in procedures will have to be based on theory, not on past experience. Experience has no predictive powers on new situations; it is useful only with similar situations. However, it remains a fact that teachers often are reluctantly passive against large doses of theory, and also that the application of theory to practice is rarely taught. This is the third way I use demonstration tapes and where I have found them very adaptive. Presented with a concrete example of a teaching situation, teachers seem to find the abstract wordiness of theoretical speculation more palatable; no doubt also because it forces the instructor to discuss theory in terms of specific examples. The majority of these discussions of theory and its application probably take place most naturally during the class discussions of the students' practice teaching VT sessions but by accident we stumbled on the following technique.

One student's micro-lesson turned out to be a veritable goldmine of various classes of drills. I had a type-written script made from the tape, presented the class with the transcript and asked them to identify the various drills in terms of whether they were mechanical, meaningful, or communicative.[2] This of course led to an extensive discussion of a theoretical classification of drills. This particular class, all experienced teachers, had earlier in the year objected rather vociferously to 'too much theory', and I remember asking them what we were doing now, theory or practice. To a man they chorused 'Practice!' no doubt pleased that I had given up my foolish ways with theory. They were of course deeply engrossed in theoretical speculation, but what they meant was that it seemed practical to them; they could see the application of it in their hand. We then viewed and discussed the tape again in terms of theory, but applied to a particular situation.

The use of VT in combination with micro-lessons in practice-teaching has certainly achieved — at least in the literature — more attention than other uses of VT. There are discussions of directed change of teacher behavior as the expected terminal behavior of VT use, and of the definite achievements of these objectives. No doubt because of my own experience, I remain rather doubtful of these claims. There are no measurements in my field that I know of which will objectively measure specific change in behavior. And I know of no experiments which particularly isolate VT in teacher training as the causal factor in behavior change. I mention this as I want to be quite clear in not making any claims that at present are not supportable. The extensive use of VT necessary to establish change in teacher behavior is simply not practical in a methods course. However, let me add the cameraman's comment about this. 'Well,' said he, 'I don't know about that, but I certainly see change in your behavior. Weren't you dead set

against this to begin with?' He was quite right; I had initially been very negative about the use of VT.

But there are certain claims we can make. All my student-teachers'
evaluations agreed that VT definitely contributed to a sense of self-image, of
self-realization. They were able to compare their micro-lessons with the
'standard lessons' they had watched in the demonstration viewings without
the distraction of simultaneously running a class. As one of them put it, we
may not actually achieve a change of behavior but certainly self-awareness
is the first step in directed change. This self-awareness seems to be a natural
result from watching oneself on VT.

But this leads us to what is probably the most important concept an
instructor of teachers can instill in his student-teachers. Perfection of
techniques and solutions to problems are important, but they are not the
most important objective. There will be new techniques and new problems
when the student-teacher is far from the help he can find in the methods
class. The most important concept a methods instructor can teach his students is to objectively and analytically examine their own teaching as a
matter of course. It is not enough that the instructor criticize and help the
students improve their teaching. They must be taught to criticize and
improve their own teaching by themselves. For this particular objective I
find VT invaluable. It is not particularly difficult to teach the techniques of
classroom teaching evaluation: demonstration films and one-way glass do
very well for this. But to instill a positive attitude of self-criticism is very
difficult. To be able to see oneself teach without the distraction of the classroom, to discuss particular activities with other colleagues in terms of practical application of theory, to be involved in group dynamics where the
expected behavior is to analyze and discuss all teaching are factors which
have in my experience been the most efficient in bringing about such an
attitude.

We use a certain ordered set of procedures, but first various decisions
of a technical nature have to be made. Whether to film in the studio or classroom, whether to film a micro-lesson or part of a regular lesson, whether to
use cameramen or stationary cameras, whether to use volunteer guinea-pig
students or the teachers' own students are the most basic problems. Generally speaking, the objectives for using the VT are the best criteria for making
procedural decisions. For example, for a demonstration film or tape it does
not matter if the teacher feels the teaching situation is artificial; we want to
depict soundness of techniques. If cameramen and a studio give better
results technically, that's what we decide on. But if the objective is a novice's
self-realization of his teaching, the decision may well be stationary cameras

and no cameramen, the real classroom and part of the real class rather than a studio situation. The truly technical problems are best left for the technician, but only after the purpose of the video-taping has been very carefully explained. If a particular type of drill is to be demonstrated, student response becomes very important and will necessitate a certain type of microphone over another. The technician must know the intended use of the VT in order to make his decisions.

Step by step, this is how we worked out a Video Tape Practice Teaching Cycle. For optimum results, the cycle should be repeated.

Step One. The initial assignment can either be given on a specific teaching point like *any–none,* or else the student-teachers may be asked to choose their own teaching point. They should have very specific directions on how to plan their micro-lesson; this is not the place for a test in writing lesson plans.

Step Two. I check over the lesson plan with each student. They appreciate the opportunity to make sure their lessons look sound on paper. This is particularly true of the non-native speakers.

Step Three. Next we video-tape the lessons. We have found 7–9 minute lessons the optimum time for getting into stride while trying to economize on time.

Step Four. Next we rerun the recorded lessons but only for the teachers taped. Actually we let the guinea-pig students watch as a 'thank you' for their participation, but at this point there is never any discussion of the lessons. Occasionally I am not even present. The objective is for the teachers to make their own analysis and comments on their own teaching, to be able to view their performance comparatively peacefully before the onslaught of a class discussion. These comments serve later to introduce each particular session: it seems only fair that a teacher gets the first chance to comment on his own teaching. It is typical that the more expert the teacher, the more critical his own comments on his teaching. These analyses are handed in as a written assignment, and compared with my own comments, it gives me a fairly good idea of how each particular student is progressing in his self-analysis as well as in his teaching.

Step Five. Next all the tapes are rerun, each teacher introducing his own lesson. Self deprecation is not encouraged. The entire class is encouraged to identify successful features as well as particular problems. In order to direct the discussion, the entire class is given a checklist for each lesson. The teacher introduces his lesson; we run the tape while the class fill in their checklists. I may comment or even stop the tape at a particularly interesting point, or else we run each micro-lesson straight through and then the class discusses the lesson. There is often disagreement which leads into theoretical discussions of language teaching pedagogy. This step is very time-consuming but worth every minute. Unless the class overlooks a significant point, I stay out of this discussion as much as possible. The class is learning to analyze and evaluate by themselves. It is a heuristic process and should not be marred by an omniscient instructor pontificating *ex cathedra*. At the end I sum up, comment and ask the teacher if he wants to make any further comments. One inviolable rule is that the teacher whose class is under discussion has lost all right to speak after his introduction unless specifically asked to do so. The reason is, of course, that the discussion easily turns into self-justification, and if the possibility for this is removed objective self-analysis is hastened. One teacher asked to comment on the criticism of his teaching, said flatly that he disagreed with me. I had said that it seemed to me the teacher spoke more than the students and he objected strenuously to this. I asked the class what they thought we should do next since the disagreement was, after all, a question of fact. Someone suggested that we run a Flanders, which we did, and I was delighted to be proved wrong. This sort of situation, I think, demonstrates more efficiently than any amount of words, that you can isolate a problem, that you can and should deal objectively with it rather than impressionistically, and on the basis of data take necessary measures. I also think it vital that the instructor can demonstrate that he too can be wrong, that he expects this to be so and that he himself anlayze and admit it. Nothing I know irritates student-teachers more than an instructor who won't admit to flaws in his own teaching.

Personal comments are never allowed in the discussion. We firmly acknowledge that teaching is ultimately an art and that we are not here to comment on each other's God-given talents. We are working on procedures and techniques, and the discussion is limited to that. A comment like 'The class seemed bored because the teacher used too many mechanical drills' is entirely legitimate; it is a procedural comment. 'The class seemed bored because the teacher didn't come across' is not allowed. If the matter of discussion is a question of an unpleasant personality such comments are not helpful; if it is a procedural problem, I want to know what it is. The instructor has to be very firm on this in the beginning, but the class very quickly catches on and will shortly not accept such comments.

Occasionally there are snags. One of the brightest students in one class did an abominable lesson, lecturing all the while on a most dubious grammatical explanation, and was promptly taken to task by the class. He gave a stirring and angry performance of self-defense and justification (after that lesson, the Rule). I was astounded by his inability to analyze his own teaching, but I was also depressed that I had apparently taught him nothing. At such a point it seems best to just go on to the next lesson and forget about the maverick. I later asked the maverick to my office and asked him how he could have been so stubborn. This is what he answered, 'I know what should be done and the others did it and I couldn't and I felt ashamed and that is why I said the things I did'. Self-awareness is the first step to change.

Step Six. The student-teachers hand in their observation charts of the lessons. It gives me a very good idea just how far along they are in being able to analyze the techniques and procedures of a language lesson. They are not graded on these, of course. The teachers can see the comments on their individual lessons if they want to.

Step Seven. The students write a reaction-evaluation report on the VT experiences. These are not graded either since they are for my benefit, and honesty is more useful than cant. I discuss their comments in class and together we agree on improved procedures for next term's class. They know and I know that the procedure just outlined is far from perfect, but they also know that they are actively helping in making it better, and they all agree that no matter how traumatic an experience, it is worth doing.

Notes

1. Since different institutions divide the various elements in a foreign language teacher training program into various combinations, I use the 'methods course' here as a generic term for theoretical aspects, techniques and procedures, practice teaching, materials adaptation and production, audio-visual aids, all of which should be included somewhere in a teacher's program.
2. For a definition of these terms, see the preceding chapter in this volume.

4 Teaching the Culturally Different Pupil

A classroom teacher's job is one of the most taxing in the world: not only must he be knowledgeable about his subject and prepared for his classes, but the sheer psychic energy which is needed to deal with lively children and adolescents all day long is rarely recognized except by other classroom teachers. The task of the teacher in schools that include among the students children from other cultures is doubly difficult. Furthermore, when those cultures in addition represent minority groups with a long tradition of social and economic exploitation by white middle-class Americans, the classroom situation often becomes unbearably difficult. These children often are slow to learn, they don't read at the national expected levels, they are late and don't do their homework, they are quiet and noisy and hostile and so on. Often these allegations are true and when the children don't learn, the teachers are blamed. The teachers become the public scapegoat for all our social ills, for the problems of the schools merely reflect the problems and social injustices of the larger society which are totally beyond the control of an individual classroom teacher. Still, a good teacher can make a tremendous difference in a child's life, and there are pieces of information which will facilitate the teaching of these culturally different children. If, for example, all reading teachers had a knowledge of black phonology, it would be a different ball game. But until we reach utopia, here are a few considerations for teaching which are designed to increase the probability of survival in the classroom — both the student's and the teacher's.

1. Culturally different, not culturally deprived

Do understand that there is no such a thing as a culturally deprived child (by culture we mean the consistent value systems and beliefs held by a group, or simply that group's unified way of looking at the world). There are culturally different children, yes, but they have a perfectly good culture of their own and in all likelihood one they prefer to mainstream American. Even though the objective of the United States public schools quite legitimately is the socialization of children into mainstream American cultural values — and remember, no one is more for this than the parents — socialization need not entail the denial of their own culture, so often accompanied by self-hate.

2. Different language, not wrong language

Do understand that the language these children speak — or dialect, and this is as true of lower-class whites as of lower-class blacks — is as perfectly good a linguistic system as the teacher's standard English; it is just different. To deny that 'ain't' is a word, or to claim that 'I ain't got no book' really means that you have got a book because two negatives make a positive, is nonsense only an English teacher could come up with. This doesn't mean that you shouldn't teach standard English, only that you should do so without disparaging the child's own mother tongue. He learned his way of talking at home, after all, and by making clear you don't like it, what you are really telling him is what you think of his family. And he is more perceptive than you are; he will understand your criticism of his family background long before it ever dawns on you what you are doing. Do be careful of your comments on students' speech; language is an integral part of their sense of self and ego-identity.

3. The same moral value expressed differently

Do recognize that different cultures may share the same moral values but express them differently on the surface. To look someone straight in the eye may signal honesty and above-board dealings to a mainstream teacher, but black children have often been carefully taught to avoid direct eye contact in order to show respect. An Amerindian child will show respect by speaking softly, and the loudness of voice which satisfies his teacher is a clear sign of anger to that child. Few teachers have been exposed to a contrastive cultural etiquette, and you might well take a look at some of the entries in the bibliography, especially Burger and Abrahams & Troike, on whose work I have drawn extensively for this paper.

4. Controlling sanctions

Don't be a Puritan ethnic with these children. Different cultures use different strategies for sanctions and rewards, and to plug someone into the wrong system just doesn't work. Internalized guilt — the touchstone of the Puritan ethic — just doesn't work in a cultural system where shame is the major controlling sanction. Middle-class American children — black or white — have internalized a set of sanctions and will self-monitor their behavior, the 'you can trust them to be good' sort of thing. Other cultures such as Hispanic, Arab, and Ghetto Black control behavior with external sanctions: a boy and a girl left alone together are expected to make love from the force of their natural feelings — therefore they are not left alone; their behavior is monitored, but from without. Shame is external, and appeal to someone's non-existent guilt feelings is just more tuned-off teacher talk. Teachers are so constantly admonished never to use sarcasm in the classroom that they never resort to it except when they are angry and then it is indeed resented by American mainstream children. But in cultures where shame is a controlling sanction, verbal ridicule is a very powerful force. Many a toughie in the classroom, where his very toughness is enhanced by his unflinching attitude to the teacher's scolding, would mind very much to be made to lose face. Sarcasm is not good because it has inherent animosity and lack of goodwill, but if you can think of a loving kind of sarcasm, sarcasm with goodwill, you will find it more efficient for controlling behavior than moral lectures. I suppose we would rather call it teasing or kidding, but then we rarely think of teasing as a way of controlling behavior. One of my staff reports the following incident, 'On the fourth day of class, two Latin American students were ten minutes late. It was reported by the others that they had gone for coffee. When they came in I commented, "I hope the coffee was good", much to the amusement of the others. No one has been late since'.

5. *Maintain authority*

Be consistent and explicit in your own behavior. Lower-class children in our culture as well as Hispanic children tend to come from authoritarian homes and you do them no favor with a permissive attitude. They will take advantage of it, and lose respect for you to boot. A case in point is the sad anecdote of one of my student-teachers in Harlem who reported back in bewilderment that her students' favorite teacher was an ex-WAC who carried and used a riding-crop. Of course the children didn't like to be beaten, but they knew exactly what to expect and they didn't have to play games with her. They respected her for making them obey. Remember, these children are not culturally deprived but they are culturally different. It is very difficult (as well as tiring) to figure out what motivates specific behaviors by people in another culture, which is why it is so important that the teacher be consistent in his behavior and that he clearly outline his particular rules. The particular configuration of values on which these rules are based are not necessarily shared by all the students, and the teacher should therefore take care to explain them. Most of all, remember that a bleeding heart attitude does them no good at all and make very sure they are held to the same exacting standards as other students. Teacher expectation of pupil work is crucial in determining the quality of the work the students produce, and it is merely inverted discrimination to expect less and to let them get by with less than acceptable work.

6. *Personal interaction*

Do reassess your ways of interacting with the students. It is typical of the cultures we are talking of here, Hispanic, Arab and Ghetto Black, that people tend to relate to persons, not to abstract moral values. There is no way that I can make my Mexican students come on time by appealing to the moral value (which they don't share) of punctuality, but they certainly come on time when I explain that I feel it an insult to my worth as a teacher when they are late and if they want to express their respect for me personally (not as a teacher) they had better come on time. This kind of manipulative strategy is repugnant to many mainstream teachers but it does work since these children have been socialized initially in this manner. You can of course do as one of my staff who spends a great deal of energy on making our Persian students feel guilty, morally guilty, for cheating; she is never going to succeed but it makes her feel good to try.

7. *Awareness of students' home circumstances*
Do reevaluate kinds of assignments. There is in these cultures a certain degree of fatalism, of *mañanaism* and a concordant lack of personal responsibility. Certainly you try to encourage the growth of such responsibility, but you also recognize that other cultures do not to the degree that we do. Nobody likes to do homework, but when both the physical conditions of the home (such as large families with no possibilities for privacy, etc.) and the cultural attitudes toward unsupervised work dictate against its being done, then out-of-class assignments become counterproductive. Most students have enough study halls to get their work done if their work is supervised, so take the trouble to talk to the study hall teachers of students who have difficulties in getting their homework done. Or have them do it in your own class. Or whatever else you can think of. But don't just damn the children for being lazy and let them slide so far behind they will never catch up.

8. *Recognize other cultures*
Do give recognition in class of the value of the other culture. It is not enough just to mouth it, you need to give active demonstration of your respect. A brief language lesson each week where the students are the teacher works very well. Ask one of the regular language teachers to help you set it up. Get parents or adults to come in and discuss their occupations, and remember that everybody does not want to become middle class. It is difficult for teachers to understand that a little boy's ambition may well be to become a garbage collector like his father, but the garbage collector has just as hard a time understanding why anyone would want to become a teacher. So there is no need to present only professional occupations; there is a need to present successful (in whatever occupation) role models from minority groups. But you might want to scrounge up a woman doctor or lawyer; professional women are also a minority group. Certainly you can think of many such activities yourself as long as you remember that one of the most important things you can teach the Anglo children is a genuine interest in and respect for other cultures.

9. *Contextual constraints*
Be alert to the possibility of contextual constraints in the teaching situation. Burger (1971) tells the anecdote of a program of pre-natal care for lower-class girls in Chile. It was offered in the local school and it was a complete flop. It so happened that in Chile sitting in a classroom was associated with childish status. But social clubs were very much in and desired upper-class behavior. So instead the meetings were held in a private home with refreshments served and the program became a huge success.

Peer teaching may be a viable alternative when the teacher cannot get through to the student. Be careful with male–female relationships in pairing students for team work. Don't punish children for speaking their own language. But most of all be alert to the fact that another culture may put a very different interpretation on the same phenomenon than you do.

10. *Disturbing behaviors*
All this doesn't mean that you won't have individual aberrations, but they are difficult to spot in another culture which you are not familiar with. Don't just write off outrageous behavior as typical of X culture. You will have to do as the anthropologists and work with informants from the same culture in order to find out as much as possible about specific sets of behavior which you find disturbing.

11. *Cum grano salis*
And finally, take with a grain of salt all the good advice experts pour over you. Sincere liking and respect for all of your students is still the *sine qua non* of all good teaching, and all the good advice in the world cannot give you that if you don't have it, and if you have it you can move the earth. Don't underestimate the tremendous importance a teacher can have in individual students' lives.

Bibliography

ABRAHAMS, R. and TROIKE, R. 1972, *Language and Culture Diversity in American Education*. Prentice-Hall: New Jersey.

ALATIS, J. E. 1969, *Linguistics and the Teaching of Standard English to Speakers of Other Languages or Dialects*. Washington, DC: Georgetown University Press.

—— (ed.) 1970, *Bilingualism and Language Contact: Anthropological, Linguistic, Psychological and Sociological Aspects*. Washington, DC: Georgetown University Press.

BARATZ, J. and SHUY, R. (eds) 1969, *Teaching Black Children to Read*. Washington, DC: Center for Applied Linguistics.

BROOKS, C. 1973, *They Can Learn English*. Belmont, California: Wadsworth Publishing Co.

BURGER, H. 1971, *Ethno-Pedagogy: Cross-Cultural Teaching Techniques.* Alberquerque, New Mexico: Southwestern Cooperative Educational Laboratory.

CAZDEN, C. *et al.* 1972, *The Function of Language in the Classroom.* New York: Teachers College Press.

COLES, R. 1972, A talk with Robert Coles. *Learning.* I, 1.

FASOLD, R. and SHUY, R. (eds) 1970, *Teaching Standard English in the Inner City.* Washington, DC: Center for Applied Linguistics.

GUMPERZ, J. and HYMES, D. (eds) 1972, *Directions in Sociolinguistics.* New York: Holt, Rinehart and Winston.

GUNDERSON, D. 1970, *Language and Reading.* Washington, DC: Center for Applied Linguistics.

HALL, E. 1959, *The Silent Language.* New York: Doubleday.

—— 1966, *The Hidden Dimension.* New York: Doubleday.

HANNERZ, U. 1969, *Soulside.* New York: Columbia Press.

HORN, T. D. (ed.) 1970, *Reading for the Disadvantaged.* New York: Harcourt, Brace and World.

JACOBSON, R. (ed.) 1971, Studies in English to speakers of other languages and standard English to speakers of a non-standard dialect. *The English Record* 21, 4 (New York State English Council) April.

KOCHMAN, T. 1973, *Rappin' and Stylin' Out.* Chicago: University of Illinois Press.

SHORES, D. 1972, *Contemporary English.* New York: Lippincott.

SPOLSKY, B. (ed.) 1972, *The Language Education of Minority Children.* Rowley, Mass.: Newbury House.

WILLIAMS, F. 1970, *Language and Poverty.* Chicago: Markham.

5 Linguistic and Communicative Competence

In this paper I would like to examine the notion of communicative competence and the implications we can draw from it for language teaching. I am using the term in Dell Hymes' sense (1967, 1972 a, b, c, d) to refer to the social rules of language use, and I argue that there are important implications for language teaching in using such a concept of communicative competence rather than taking it to mean simply linguistic interaction in the target language.

The impetus for the paper came from my experience in Sweden in 1973. I spent my sabbatical leave in my home town, Stockholm, which I had left at the age of eighteen. I found that, although I was still fluent in the language, aspects of Swedish culture had become foreign to me and that I consequently failed at times to communicate efficiently. I reflected on the implications of this failure in light of my reading in sociolinguistics, and this paper attempts to formulate the significance certain sociolinguistic concepts have for language teaching. There is a section in a paper by Bernstein (1972: 55–69) which ends 'These are poorly worked out thoughts'. I should also offer such an admission here, but I want to add that I strongly feel that these are thoughts we need to work out.

Within the last five years there has been an increasing — and justified — concern for communicative activities in language teaching. We see evidence of this everywhere, in the titles of papers and articles and dissertations. In 1973 an entire conference was held in England on 'The Communicative Teaching of English'.[1] Savignon's (1971) dissertation 'Study of the effect of training in communicative skills as part of a beginning college French course on student attitude and achievement in linguistic and communicative competence' proves beyond any doubt the necessity for such activities, where 'the emphasis was always at getting meaning across' (Savignon, 1971: 24). And there's the rub; what kind of meaning? Rivers (1973: 26) uses communicative competence as a synonym for 'spontaneous expression', and it is rather typical of language teachers and psycholinguists (see, for example, Miller, 1970; Titone, 1970) that they tend to equate communicative competence with the ability to carry out linguistic interaction in the target language. As Halliday (1970: 145–6) points out, it is predominant in our thinking about language that we want it to allow us 'to communicate something. We use language to represent our experience of the processes, persons, objects, abstractions, qualities, states and relations of the world around us and inside us'. Sociolinguists and anthropologists are careful to distinguish this referential meaning of language from the social meaning language also carries. In Gumperz' (1971: 285) terms:

> effective communication requires that speakers and audiences agree both on the meaning of words and on the social import or values attached to choice of expression . . . We will use the term social significance or social meaning to refer to the social values implied when an utterance is used in a certain context.

A very large part of the criticism levelled against Chomsky concerns the inadequacy of his attempts to explain language in terms of the narrow notions of the linguistic competence of an ideal hearer-speaker in a homogeneous society. Such a speaker, says Hymes (1972d: 277) is likely to become institutionalized if he simply produces any and all of the grammatical sentences of the language with no regard for their appropriateness. John Lyons (1970: 287) sums it up:

> It is frequently suggested that there is a conflict between the sociolinguistic and the psycholinguistic approach to language; and furthermore that generative grammar (which according to Chomsky is a branch of cognitive psychology) must necessarily adopt the latter. I do not believe that this is so.
>
> The two points of view, the sociolinguistic and the psycholinguistic can certainly be distinguished at the moment (and linguists tend to favor the one or the other according to their particular interests). But ultimately they must be reconciled. The ability to use one's language correctly in a variety of socially determined situations is as much and as central a part of linguistic 'competence' as the ability to produce grammatically well-formed sentences. (Lyons, 1970: 287)

The term Hymes has suggested for a knowledge of the rules for understanding and producing both the referential and the social meaning of language is *communicative competence*. Since the publication of Gumperz & Hymes (1964) 'The ethnography of communication', a great many sociolinguists have been trying to discover and understand the rules of speaking which underlie utterances and invest them with social meaning. It is customary in the literature to point out that we are only at the beginning stages of adequate descriptive work, but we certainly are beginning to see patterned processes with inherent rules in a multitude of speech encounters, from insults and 'rapping' to systems of addressing people and switching codes. In the literature on linguistic variation and the social meaning of this variation, the term communicative competence is almost invariably used in Hymes' sense. (See, for example, Jakobovits, 1970; Osser, 1971; Kernan, 1971; Slobin, 1967; Kochman, 1973.) I find it crucial that we as language teachers do the same thing. It may seem picayune to quibble over the meaning of a term; like Alice, we could just pay it to make it mean what we want. But it isn't quibbling; it is of the utmost importance. Communicative competence is not simply a term; it is a concept basic to understanding social interaction. It is commonplace to point out that the tenets and concepts of a discipline profoundly influence the questions one asks and the solutions one seeks as well as limit the phenomena one observes. In Rivers' sense of the term I would concentrate on teaching the referential meaning of language; in Hymes' term I would go beyond to the social meaning of language. I hope to make clear why I think the social meaning is so important in language teaching.

Wardhaugh points out that:

> In each historical period an attempt is made, conscious or otherwise, to unite the prevailing knowledge of language, the prevailing understanding of language learning and the prevailing concept of education goals into a pattern of language teaching. (Wardhaugh, 1968: 81)

I think that is what we are partially trying to do in language teaching today, and which explains the interest in the notions of communicative competence. If you accept Hymes' (1972d: 278) notion that a model of language must be designed with a face toward communicative conduct and social life, then it follows that a model for teaching language must also be designed with a face toward communicative conduct and social life.

I would like to suggest a model for language teaching which sets up a framework for identifying and discussing strategies and techniques in the teaching process, taking into account the social meaning of language. The model is shown in Figure 5.1.

Prior to a discussion of the implications for language teaching, the terms, especially that of communicative performance, merit careful consideration. By linguistic competence, Chomsky means the native speaker's knowledge of his own language, the set or system of internalized rules about the language which enables him to create new grammatical sentences and to understand sentences spoken to him, to reject 'the ate goldfish John' as un-

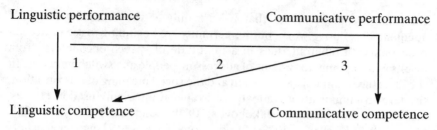

FIGURE 5.1   *A model for language teaching*

English and to recognize that 'flying planes can be dangerous' is ambiguous. Linguistic performance is the actual utterance, what the speaker actually says, which often imperfectly reflects the underlying competence (Chomsky, 1968). Communicative competence is the social rules of language use, 'the systemic sets of social interactional rules' in Grimshaw's (1973: 109) terms. I have added the notion of *communicative performance*[2] as I need a term which will designate communication which carries no distinctive social significance. In the real world this is not possible, but in the artificial world of language classrooms there are communicative activities which lack specific deep structures of social meaning. I suspect this statement needs further modification: an activity like Twenty Questions does not carry any distinctive social meaning of the specific language it is played in; the students simply function with their native rules of speaking, and whatever social meaning lies in playing Twenty Questions in Spanish, French or English comes from the social interactional rules of the subculture of the classroom, but it has nothing to do with developing communicative competence in the target language. I also need a term which can be used to describe an encounter where different social meanings are encoded in, or decoded from the same linguistic expression. In such a case we get communicative ambiguity, the same surface behavior but with the deep structures in two separate sets of communicative competence — the very opposite of Gumperz' 'efficient communication'. Let me try to clarify this with a representative anecdote. In Sweden, we celebrated Thanksgiving by having my immediate family and friends for a traditional turkey dinner. I was busy in the kitchen and came belatedly into the living room where my sister-in-law had just arrived. In impeccable Swedish I asked her politely, 'Do you know everyone?' Any native American would correctly interpret that to mean that I wanted to know if she had been introduced to those guests she had not previously met. She looked at me sourly and said, 'I don't know everyone, but if you are asking me if I have greeted everyone, I have'. Fussed as I was and in such an archetypical American situation, I had momentarily forgotten that proper manners demand that Swedes do not wait to be introduced by a third party, but go around the room, shake hands with everyone and say their name aloud to those they have not previously met. Any child knows that, and my sister-in-law felt I had reprimanded her for bad manners, her faulty sharing of a systemic set of social interactional rules. Clearly, the meaning of an interaction is easily misinterpreted if the speakers don't share the same set of rules, as in this example of noneffective communication where the same surface structure carried different social meaning.

In language teaching we are always dealing with cross-cultural encounters, and what typically happens is that the student applies his native rules of speaking to the target language, rules which may imply a very different social significance. Here is another anecdote from my Swedish visit. Americans ask many questions, often of a rather personal nature,[3] and they are also (presumably as a consequence) very skilled at avoiding answering questions. This is simply an accepted part of communicative competence. On a superficial level, communicative competence may simply be defined as tact and good manners, and people not sharing that same system will consider others rude and tactless, just as the stereotyped American is considered rude and tactless in Europe. Well, in Sweden I asked a question of a confidential family matter that I expected not to be answered; to my surprise it was, only to have my family criticize me for my inexcusable tactless behavior. My answer that the question need not have been answered was totally dismissed; according to Swedish rules of speaking such questions are not asked; but according to the same rules, questions asked are answered without subterfuge. By American rules, on the contrary, you may ask but without expecting an answer. In this encounter there was nothing faulty with the linguistic aspects — we were both native speakers of Swedish — nor with the communicative performance — we both understood that I sought a piece of information — but the social significance certainly was at variance. I was applying the wrong set of rules of communicative competence.

This anecdote also illustrates another aspect of communicative competence: it is easier to keep one's linguistic codes separate than one's social codes as one often is not aware of the social codes on a conscious level until they are violated. It is much easier to be bilingual than bicultural.

So far I have said very little about teaching. Oller (1973: 7) at his satirical best points out that it is very fashionable to say that you don't know much about a topic before you go on to discuss it so that you can pass yourself off as a bit of humble genius. Still, I don't think we know very much of what really goes on in language acquisition. Empirically, however, I know what our students must do in order to learn English. I have outlined elsewhere the process of mechanical-meaningful-communicative kinds of exercises that the learner needs to go through in order to internalize the grammatical rules of the language (Paulston, 1970, 1971 — see Chapter 2, this volume). I am more convinced than ever after four months of teaching non-academic adults of the necessity of the initial stage of acquiring basic skills through habituation,[4] just as I remain convinced of the need for the communicative drills in order to internalize the rules. As Rivers (1972: 76) points out in her excellent 'Talking off the top of their heads', we next need autonomous interaction activities where the students use language for the normal purpose of language: establishing social relations, seeking and giving information, hiding one's intentions, etc. It is at this point we need to become sensitive to whether these are activities for developing communicative competence or merely exercises in communicative performance. It may well be wrong to say *merely*; it is valid to ask how much communicative competence one needs to teach in foreign language teaching. At this point we might again consider the model in Figure 5.1. I find it very dubious that Strategy 1 can be efficient in language learning. Merely practice in the rules and utterances of a language is not likely to produce fluent speakers, a fact to which both the products of the grammar-translation and classic audio-lingual methods attest. Strategy 2, which combines skill-getting exercises (drills, dialogues, rules, etc.) with skill-using activities of the kind Savignon (1971) outlines in her dissertation, will under propitious circumstances (good programs, trained teachers, motivated students) result in linguistic competence. In foreign language teaching that may be all one asks. It is the contention of this paper that the most efficient language teaching follows Strategy 3.

The necessity to develop communicative competence is especially important in second language and second dialect teaching where the fact that the speakers are using the same national language easily obscures the equally important fact that the speakers may not share the same rules for speaking. And even if this is apparent, the faulty social meaning conveyed is likely to be just tacitly registered. There are in the United States very strong constraints on teaching adults to behave. Sociolinguistic rules, it is felt, one should learn as a child, and teaching adults such rules implies that they were not 'properly' brought up. Furthermore, and I am speculating, there may well be a feeling that it is chauvinistic to correct immigrant-like behavior. In their socialization process, Americans are taught that anti-immigrant behavior is un-American. There is no corresponding attitude in Sweden, e.g. where immigrants are at times subjected to public behavior that would never be tolerated in the United States. Whatever the reasons, native American teachers are embarrassed to correct adults' improper behavior, that is, behavior with deviant social meaning which we primarily perceive as improper. However, there are two types of behavior teachers tend not to condone: the use of taboo words in inappropriate contexts and behavior which carries deviant sexual meaning; no one hesitates to inform our students that *bullshit*, a term they pick up very quickly, is not an acceptable substitute for *nonsense* in the classroom.

This constraint on teaching social rules of communicative competence is interesting in that it reveals how very deepseated our belief is that our rules are the only real ones. The constraint on correction only holds for the rules of communicative competence in the native tongue. In foreign language classrooms, American teachers have no hesitation in teaching the quaint customs of the French and the Spanish. If the inhibition on correcting adults is a universal tendency, one could use the lack of such inhibition in either language of a bilingual as an indication of the degree to which he is bicultural. I think it is important that teachers understand the constraints on their behavior towards the student. It is not rude to correct a student whose behavior you react to as deviant; I have begun to think that it is a necessary element in language teaching. The important thing to remember is not to imply any inherent moral superiority of one rule over another, to remember the difference between adding rules and substituting rules. In the latter case, one obviously rejects the value of the first set of rules, rejects the very culture of the student. However, it gives a skewed picture not to make very clear here that the emphasis should be on *teaching* communicative behavior, not on correcting forms which deviate from it.

In the matter of second language or second dialect speakers, the teaching situation is likely to be that of the public schools, where the constraint on correcting deviant behavior does not hold: indeed, some teachers see it as their major task. But the teacher's belief that his rules of communicative competence are the only real and acceptable rules remains exactly as invariable, and with the constraints on correction removed, there is no hesitation here in making this belief explicit. I pointed out in an article several years ago that the process of learning a foreign and a second language might be a very different psychological experience (Paulston, 1972). I now think that this difference between learning a foreign and a second language stems from the social meaning of the L2. The communicative competence rules of a Chicano Spanish speaker are likely to include the social significance of using English even before he can speak a word of it. By itself, there is nothing wrong in this; a Moroccan boy will also have rules for the social meaning of classical Arabic long before he can speak it. In the latter case, everything he learns in learning classical Arabic supports his self-development, his sense of ego, his father's values. It is the process of trying to eradicate an existing set of social interactional rules in order to substitute another which is so counterproductive in language teaching. We are at present puzzled by the fact that upper and middle-class children suffer no ill effect from initial schooling in the L2 while lower-class children do. It may well be that there is no attempt to interfere with the rules for communicative competence of the upper-class children — this would mean, for example, the St Lambert's (Lambert & Tucker, 1972) children speak French but with the rules of speaking they originally learned for English — while with the lower-class children one insists that they adopt the social interactional rules of the target language. I am merely speculating, but it should demonstrate that using Hymes' concept of communicative competence we can begin to ask some searching questions.[5]

It should be clear, then, that the implications for language teaching that we can draw from the notions of communicative competence apply primarily to situations where the learners live in the country of the target language, whether they are second-language speakers or foreign students.

Well, what do we teach? When we teach 'How do you do' in the first lesson, we better also teach that it is only used in face to face encounters, and when we later do telephone conversations we can easily contrast the 'Hello, this is John Doe' with 'How do you do, I am John Doe'. Of course, situational teaching has always included aspects of this but what we need to do is incorporate a systematic contrast of situational constraints on grammatical patterns.

We also need to incorporate teaching situational constraints on register variation. Many expressions which are socially inappropriate in English are caused by register interference. The Spanish speaker's *Dios mio* does not carry the same meaning as 'My God', but how is he to know that it is not a harmless expletive in English unless he is told so. We also need to teach our students to be sensitive to levels of style so that noting such levels becomes part of their language learning strategies. We run our students through dialogues like these:

Variations on a Theme # 1
Last weekend Bill went to see a very popular movie, starring one of his favorite actors and a beautiful young actress. He's discussing it with Nancy.
Nancy: Hey, Bill. What did you do over the weekend?
Bill: Saw the new flick with Peck and Welch.
Nancy: Oh, yeah? How was it?
Bill: Peck was great as usual, and well, you don't go to see great acting from Raquel.
Nancy: Know what you mean. All the guys go to watch Raquel. For me Peck is the drawing card. Gotta go to class — see you later.

Bill: So long.

On the way home on the bus, Bill sits next to a lady who lives down the street. She is a good friend of Bill's parents.

Mrs Cassetti: Did you have a pleasant weekend, Bill?

Bill: Yes, thank you. I studied quite a bit, but Saturday I took the evening off and went to the new movie with Gregory Peck and Raquel Welch.

Mrs Cassetti: Oh, did you? Did you enjoy it?

Bill: Gregory Peck was very good — he always is. Raquel Welch isn't expected to be a great actress, I guess.

Mrs Cassetti: Yes, I suppose you're right. All of the young men certainly seem to enjoy her movies. From my point of view Gregory Peck would be the reason for going. I have to get off here. It was nice to see you, Bill.

Bill: It was nice talking to you. Goodbye, Mrs Cassetti.

(Bruder, 1973)

We need to teach the small talk of such situations which tend to use phatic language: greetings, introductions, farewells. The students need to stand up and do introductions, greetings, etc. The nonverbal aspects of language are exceedingly important. I told my Swedish students, for instance, that in English it is the woman who first extends her hand in greeting — the reverse of Swedish — and that a man has to be prepared for the possibility that a woman will not shake hands with him, a very difficult point to learn for speakers from hand-shaking cultures. My students had lots of fun doing those.

How is the teacher going to know that such rules are needed? The difficulty with so many rules of communicative competence is that we don't consciously know many of our own, much less those of another culture. This is where the teacher becomes an anthropologist, by listening to students, observing behavior and most of all by being aware and alert to possible conflicts. Over the years you amass quite a few rules; in the English Language Institute we even have a rule which says adult males don't walk hand in hand in the streets, courtesy of our Libyan students.

There are several classroom techniques for teaching communicative competence, and I discuss those in Chapter 6.

Notes

1. *The Communicative Teaching of English.* AILA/BAAL Seminar, University of Lancaster, March 30 — April 1, 1973. Program Chairman, Christopher Candlin.
2. I know full well that this is not in keeping with Hymes' framework.

3. But note that what exactly constitutes a personal question is culturally determined. However much Swedes look askance at American questioning behavior, they are not unlikely to inquire of a friend the amount of his salary. I am here referring to questions about number of children, kind of occupation, place of birth, etc.
4. Rivers uses the more elegant term cognition to refer to this stage. We both, however, refer to the same initial stage of acquiring basic knowledge of 'units, categories, and functions'. 'Through habituation' is of course a moot point, but I am in good company, see John Carroll, 'Current issues in psycholinguistics and second language teaching', *TESOL Quarterly*, 5, 2 (June, 1971), 101–14.
5. This speculation — as later classroom research in Canada showed — turned out to be highly accurate.

References

BERNSTEIN, B. 1972, Elaborated and restricted codes: their origin and consequences. In J. GUMPERZ and D. HYMES (eds) *Directions in Sociolinguistics*. New York: Holt, Rinehart and Winston.

BRUDER, M. N. 1973, *MMC: Developing Communicative Competence in English as a Second Language*. Pittsburgh: English Language Institute.

CHOMSKY, N. 1968, *Language and Mind*. New York: Harcourt, Brace and World.

GRIMSHAW, A. D. 1973, Rules, social interaction, and language behavior. *TESOL Quarterly* 7, 2.

GUMPERZ, J. 1971, *Language in Social Groups*. Stanford: Stanford University.

GUMPERZ, J. and HYMES, D. (eds) 1964, The ethnography of communication. *American Anthropologist* 66, 6, 2.

HALLIDAY, M. A. K. 1970, Language structure and language function. In J. LYONS (ed.) *New Horizons in Linguistics*. Harmondsworth, England: Penguin Books.

HYMES, D. 1967, The anthropology of communication. In F. DANCE (ed.) *Human Communication Theory*. New York: Holt, Rinehart and Winston.

—— 1972a, Editorial introduction. *Language and Society* 1, 1, 1–14.

—— 1972b, Introduction. In C. CAZDEN, V. JOHN and D. HYMES (eds) *The Function of Language in the Classroom*. New York: Teachers College Press.

—— 1972c, Models of the interaction of language and social life. In J. GUMPERZ and D. HYMES (eds) *Directions in Sociolinguistics*. New York: Holt, Rinehart and Winston.

—— 1972d, On communicative competence. In J. B. PRIDE and J. HOLMES (eds) *Sociolinguistics*. Harmondsworth, England: Penguin Books.

JAKOBOVITS, L. 1970, Prolegomena to a theory of communicative competence. In R. C. LUGTON (ed.) *English as a Second Language*. Philadelphia: Center for Curriculum Development.

KERNAN, C. M. 1971, Response. In *Sociolinguistics: A Crossdisciplinary Perspective*. Washington, DC: Center for Applied Linguistics.

KOCHMAN, T. 1973, *Rappin' and Stylin' Out*. Chicago: University of Illinois Press.

LAMBERT W. and TUCKER, R. 1972, *Bilingual Education of Children*. Rowley, Mass.: Newbury House.

LYONS, J. (ed.) 1970, *New Horizons in Linguistics*. Harmondsworth, England: Penguin Books.

MILLER, G. 1970, The psycholinguists. In M. LESTER (ed.) *Readings in Applied Transformational Grammar*. New York: Holt, Rinehart and Winston.

OLLER J. 1973, Pragmatic language testing. *Language Sciences* 28.

OSSER, H. 1971, Developmental studies of communicative competence. In *Sociolinguistics: A Crossdisciplinary Perspective*. Washington, DC: Center for Applied Linguistics.

PAULSTON, C. B. 1970, Structural pattern drills: A classification. *Foreign Language Annals* 4, 2, 187–93.

—— 1971, The sequencing of structural pattern drills. *TESOL Quarterly* 5, 3, 197–208.

—— 1972, Las escuelas bilingues in Peru. *IRAL* 10, 4, 351–5.

RIVERS, W. 1972, Talking off the top of their heads. *TESOL Quarterly* 6, 1.

—— 1973, From linguistic competence to communicative competence. *TESOL Quarterly* 7, 1.

SAVIGNON, S. 1971, Study of the effect of training in communicative skills as part of a beginning college French course on student attitude and achievement in linguistic and communicative competence. Unpublished Ph.D. dissertation. University of Illinois.

SLOBIN, D. 1967, *A Field Manual for Cross-cultural Study of the Acquisition of Communicative Competence*. University of California at Berkeley. (Mimeo.)

TITONE, R. 1970, A psycholinguistic model of grammar learning and foreign language. In R. C. LUGTON (ed.) *English as a Second Language: Current Issues*. Philadelphia, Center for Curriculum Development.

WARDHAUGH, R. 1968, Linguistics, psychology, and pedagogy: trinity or unity. *TESOL Quarterly* 2, 2.

6 Developing Communicative Competence: Goals, Procedures and Techniques

Introduction

When I first discussed my participation here today at the Lackland Defense Language Institute, I was told categorically, 'Nothing theoretical'. I have tried very hard to keep to the spirit of those instructions, and as a consequence, I have barely touched on the theoretical assumptions on which this paper is based.[1] I have done so elsewhere (Paulston, 1974: see Chapter 5) and you should be aware that there exists a considerable literature on the theoretical aspects of communicative competence. But today I want to discuss the practical implications, as I see them, for language teaching, and to share with you the work my colleagues and I are doing in the English Language Institute of the University of Pittsburgh, which has a teaching situation fairly similar to yours.[2]

Virtually everyone agrees that the creative aspect of language is neglected in the audio-lingual method, and that this is an important element of language learning. There is fairly unanimous agreement on the need for communication *within* the language teaching process. The key word has become communicative competence, and that is what I want to talk about today: what it is, why we teach it and specifically how we teach it.

Communicative Competence

Generally, communicative competence is taken to be the objective of language teaching (as such it fits right into the audio-lingual tradition): the production of speakers competent to communicate in the target language. As Frank Johnson has pointed out, communication

requires interpersonal responsiveness, rather than the mere production of language which is truthful, honest, accurate, stylistically pleas-
ing, etc., those characteristics which look at language rather than as
behavior, which is the social purpose of language. Our end product is
surely getting things done, easing social tensions, goading ourselves
into doing this or that, and persuading others to do things. Communication arises when language is used as such interpersonal behavior,
which goes beyond meaningful and truthful manipulation of language
symbols. (Johnson, 1970)

It is when we try to isolate the skills we need for efficient communication that we find divergent opinions. It is rather typical of language teachers
that they tend to equate communicative competence with the ability to carry
out linguistic interaction in the target language — River's lecture here last
year is a good example of this approach (Rivers, 1973). But efficient communication requires also that speakers share the social meaning of the linguistic forms, that they have the same social rules for language use. Dell
Hymes, the anthropologist, argues that communicative competence must
include not only the linguistic forms of a language but also a knowledge of
when, how and to whom it is appropriate to use these forms (see Chapter 5).
I have argued elsewhere the necessity of defining communicative competence as Hymes does, and I won't do that here, but notice that I am using
the term in a slightly different sense from what you have heard before. I have
come to think that it is every bit as important that we teach the appropriate
forms of social usage as the linguistic forms themselves. Let me give you
some examples. We all teach the wh-questions early in the curriculum, but
we don't teach the questions you can and cannot ask. If you were to ask me
what form of birth control I practice, I would probably consider you drunk,
somewhat mad, or incredibly rude. Yet David Eskey tells me he was frequently asked that question in Thailand. The social meaning of the same
linguistic form varies from culture to culture. Communication includes non-
verbal behavior as well; as often cited, eye contact behavior carries the
meaning of honest dealings in Anglo culture while it is rude and disrespectful
in Hispanic as well as in many other cultures. You probably all know that,
but how many of you have taught 'proper' (and I'll come back to that) eye
contact behavior to your students? You should realize that there are very
strong constraints on teaching adults to behave. Sociolinguistic rules, it is
felt, should be learned in childhood, and teaching adults such rules implies
that they were not properly brought up. Obviously, however, there is
nothing inherently more proper about one set of behavior *vis-à-vis* another
except in cultural appropriateness. On a superficial level, communicative

competence may simply be defined as tact and good manners, and people not sharing that system will consider others rude and tactless. We do our students a disservice if we don't teach them the social rules along with the linguistic rules as long as we remember not to imply any moral superiority of one rule over the other.

Occasionally, faulty rule sharing will lead to complete breakdown in communication. Here is an example from my recent stay in Sweden, where I was born and raised. We (my American husband and children) celebrated Thanksgiving by having my immediate family (Swedish) and friends for a traditional turkey dinner. I was busy in the kitchen and came belatedly into the living room where my sister-in-law had just arrived. In impeccable Swedish I asked her politely, 'Do you know everyone?' Any native American would correctly interpret such a question to mean that I wanted to know if she had been introduced to those guests she had not previously met. She looked at me sourly and said, 'I don't know everyone, but if you are asking me if I have greeted everyone, I have'. Fussed as I was, and in such an archetypical American situation, I had momentarily forgotten that proper manners demand that Swedes do not wait to be introduced by a third party, but go around the room, shake hands with everyone and say their name aloud to those they have not previously met. Any child knows that, so my sister-in-law felt I had reprimanded her for bad manners, for faulty sharing of a systemic set of social interactional rules. Clearly, the meaning of an interaction is easily misinterpreted if the speakers don't share the same set of rules. Hence the necessity for teaching those rules.

This anecdote also illustrates another aspect of communicative competence: it is easier to keep one's linguistic codes separate than one's social codes as one is often not aware of the social codes on a conscious level until they are violated. It is much easier to be bilingual than bicultural.

Communicative Competence: Goals

It is important to be clear about the goals of teaching communicative competence because the techniques and procedures of teaching follow from these goals. Linguistic competence forms part of communicative competence, so our students need just as always to acquire a basic knowledge of linguistic forms, the skill-getting stage in Rivers' (1972) model. Your regular course-work will serve perfectly well for this stage. The teaching points here can be broken down to specific sounds, grammar patterns and vocabulary items in the traditional skills of listening, speaking, reading and writing.

But learning specific sounds and patterns does not necessarily entail the ability to use them, and our students need practice in using the linguistic forms for the social purpose of language, as Johnson describes it. You will remember Rivers discussing with you the need for students to use language for the normal purposes of language: establishing social relations, seeking and giving information, etc. (Rivers, 1973). There is enough experimental evidence that this is a necessary step in efficient language learning, and so it must be incorporated in the teaching process as well. You need to be certain that such interaction activities form part of your curriculum on a frequent and regular basis, in beginning courses as well as in advanced.

There are two basic classes of communicative interaction activities, depending on the teaching point, and there is room for both in the curriculum. In one kind of exercises, the teaching point is simply to get meaning across, to be able to communicate some referential meaning in the target language. These I have called exercises in communicative performance, and they are excellent and necessary for developing linguistic competence. In the other type of exercises the teaching point is getting meaning across in a socially acceptable way, and typically these exercises contain culturally relevant information, social interactional rules, in what I at times call a contrastive Emily Post approach to language teaching. Only the latter I would call activities for developing communicative competence.

I will discuss procedures and techniques with each specific type of interaction activity, but there is one set of procedures which holds for all of the communicative interaction activities, and which I cannot emphasize strongly enough. There should be *no* correction from the teacher during these activities. If the basic teaching point is getting meaning across, the students have achieved the objectives of the exercise if they succeed in doing so. It is inhibiting, hampering and frustrating beyond belief to be consistently checked and corrected when one is struggling with ideas in another language. On the other hand, the teacher helps with vocabulary, grammar and pronunciation, when the students ask him as they frequently do. The students should very early on be taught phrases for talking themselves out of trouble: phrases like 'How do you say this in English?', 'Is that right?', 'What's the word for the thing that . . . ?' are very useful to know. What we do in the Institute is that the teacher writes down the worst horrors he hears, and then the class spends five or ten minutes after the exercise in a friendly post mortem. We concentrate on clearing up idiom and vocabulary confusion, and it is elementary psychology but nevertheless effective to point out *good* word choices and expressions too. Once in a blue moon you run across a student who insists that the teacher correct his every mistake; you are likely to lose his confidence if you don't, so the easiest way out is to tape his performance and then go over it with him outside of class. But it is too inhibiting, time-consuming and inefficient to tape record these activities for correction purposes as a standard procedure for the whole class.

Communicative Interaction Activities

In the Institute, we use four basic types of activities in various combinations for developing communicative competence: social formulas and dialogues, community oriented tasks, problem-solving activities, and role-play. There are surely others, but we have not thought of any. I am deliberately excluding from this discussion exercises in communicative performance, such as games and charades although we use them too.

Social formulas and dialogues

Judy Kettering (1975) in her *Interaction Activities* has one unit on 'Establishing and maintaining social relations' which covers such speech encounters as greetings, partings, introductions, excuses, compliments, complaints, hiding feelings, etc. It is very difficult to lie, to complain, and to turn someone down for a date in another language, and our students need to be taught how to do this in an appropriate manner. These are exercises deliberately designed to develop communicative competence as you can see from this section on 'Excuses and apologies' (Kettering, 1975: 22).

Excuses and Apologies
(abbreviated)

I.   Phrases

    A. Formal

        1.   Excuse me, please.
            Pardon me.   Of course.
            I'm very sorry.   Certainly.
            I'm sorry.
            I beg your pardon.

        2.   Excuse me for being late.   ⎧ That's quite alright. ⎫
            I'm sorry I'm late.   ⎨   ⎬
            Excuse me for a moment please.   ⎩ Think nothing of it. ⎭

            ⎧ I'm sorry I forgot to ⎫ ⎧ call.   ⎫
            ⎩ I'm sorry I didn't   ⎭ ⎨ come.   ⎬
                                ⎪ answer your letter. ⎪
                                ⎩ inform you.   ⎭
            I'm sorry, but I must leave early.

B. Informal

    2. Sorry I'm late.

      Sorry I forgot to { call. / write. / come. / tell you. }

      Just a minute. I'll be right back.

    { It's OK. / Don't worry. / Sure. }

    { It's alright. }

II. Dialogues

  A. Formal

    2. **A:** Miss Larson?
       B: Yes?
       A: Please excuse me for losing my temper in class yesterday.
       B: That's quite alright. Was something troubling you?
       A: Yes. I had just gotten a letter from a friend of mine and I guess I was more upset than I thought.

  B. Informal

    1. **A:** How was your vacation, Maria?
       B: I had such a good time, I hated to come back.
       A: Did you get my postcard?
       B: Yes, thanks. And I meant to write to you too but I was just so busy! I'm sorry.
       A: That's OK. I knew you probably didn't have much time.

    3. **A:** I'm glad you're still here! Sorry I'm so late.
       B: Don't worry. The bus hasn't come yet.
       A: I was just walking out the door and the phone rang. It was my mother and . . . well, you know how my mother talks!
       B: I'm surprised you aren't later!

III. Situations

  A. Structured

    1. **A:** How was your vacation?
       B: Great. Hey, thanks for the postcards.
       A: Sure. But I didn't get any from you!
       B:

  B. Semi-Structured

    1. **A:** Hey, where were you last night?
       B: I was waiting for you to call to tell me what the address was.

> **A:**
> **B:**
>
> 2. **A:** What'd you get so angry at me for this morning?
>   **B:**
>   **A:**
>   **B:**

C. Unstructured

1. You're in class and suddenly you don't feel well.

4. You are at a friend's house for dinner. You must leave early to study for a test for the next day.

6. You told Fred you would come over to study with him last night, but you forgot. He sees you and asks you why you didn't come.

In all of these activities, there is a progression from tightly controlled language use, where the student is learning the social formulas to a situation where he can use them. The phrases and the dialogues lend themselves well to work in the language laboratory, but it is important that the teacher spends some time in the initial presentation of the section in explaining the meaning, the connotations, and the sorts of situations in which you would use the various expressions, an introductory mixture of Emily Post and sociolinguistics as it were. I was amazed to see the eagerness with which our students received this information; it clearly filled a definite need. Note section IB. In all of these encounters, the students are taught a formal and an informal way for apologizing, saying thank you, etc. I doubt that one can systematically teach register variation in all areas of language, but we *can* teach our students to be sensitive to levels of style so that noting such levels becomes part of their language learning strategies.

Although the dialogues can be assigned to the lab, they lend themselves well to pupil-to-pupil work, where the whole class is divided into pairs working simultaneously. The students in each pair take turns reading from the printed dialogue while the other answers from memory until they can run through both parts of the dialogue without looking at the text. This old technique is a remarkably quick way for a class to memorize brief dialogues.[3]

The *Situations* (from structured to unstructured) take on aspects of play-acting or role-play and are more effective with an audience. The unstructured situations lend themselves particularly well to role-play and are best handled as such. (See discussion under role-play.)

Community oriented tasks

Community Oriented Tasks (Kettering, 1975: 39–50) are sets of exercises which compel the student to interact with native speakers outside the classroom. The teaching point here is twofold: (1) communicative participation in the community, and (2) (and this is what assures their success) the collection of highly relevant and needed information. Here are two examples:

The bank

1. What is a checking account? A savings account?
2. Can you take money out of a savings account at any time?
3. What is interest? What bank gives the highest interest rate in Oakland? What is 'compounding' of interest? What is the difference between interest compounded daily, monthly, quarterly, bi-annually, annually? Which gives you the most money?
4. What does 'withdrawal' mean? 'Deposit'?
5. What is 24-hour banking? Does the Oakland Pittsburgh National Bank (next to the Book Center) have 24-hour banking?
6. How do you open an account?
7. If you take out a loan, do you want a high interest rate or a low interest rate? Why?
8. There are three types of checking accounts:
   a. minimum balance
   b. 10¢ a check
   c. free checking
   What are the differences between these three kinds? Advantages and disadvantages?
9. What happens if you 'overdraw'?
10. What other services do banks provide besides the above?

The automobile

1. What are Service Stations?
   What is 'regular' gasoline? 'super'? 'low-lead'?
   How much does each cost per gallon?
   How much does a quart of oil cost?
2. How often must you have your car inspected? How much does it cost?
3. What is a 'tune-up'? How often should your car be 'tuned up'? How often should you change oil? What must you put in the water in your car in the winter?
4. Do you need a US driver's license to own a car? Where do you get a driver's license? What tests do you have to take to get a license? How long is a license valid? How much does it cost?

5. What is automobile insurance? What are the differences between the following kinds of automobile insurance?
   a. comprehensive
   b. collision
   c. uninsured driver
   Why is it a good idea to have insurance? Where do you get insurance?
6. Buying a car:
   a. What is a warranty?
   b. Is the purchase of a car taxable?
   c. Can you usually trust car salesmen? Why or why not?
   d. What is a 'test drive'?
   e. What is car registration? Where should it be kept?
7. If you get stuck on a highway or freeway (your car breaks down), what should you do?
8. What is AAA? What services does it offer?

The assignment is handed out in class, and the topic explained in general terms. Then it is up to the students to find the answers outside of class. After a reasonable amount of time, they report their findings to the rest of the class. An alternative to oral reports is to have them act out their answers in a role-play, like this one:

Role-playing: The bank

Situation:

Alfred Newman has just moved to Pittsburgh and has gone to the Pittsburgh National Bank to open both a checking account and a savings account. He must answer questions asked by a bank employee who types out the information. He has a check for $5,000 which he wants to put in the savings account and his first pay check for $289.35 with which he will open the checking account.

Roles:

Alfred Newman — young man who has just moved to Pittsburgh.
Tilda Thompson — bank employee.

Useful expressions:

Alfred: 'I just moved to Pittsburgh.'
   'I would like to open a bank account.'
   'I have two checks to deposit.'
Tilda: 'Good morning. May I help you?'
   'I need your name, address, etc.'

'Let me have your checks and I'll deposit them for you and bring your receipts.'
'What type of checking account do you want?'

Information necessary to open bank accounts:

A. Checking account
   1. Name, address, phone number.
   2. Occupation and employer.
   3. Individual or joint (with wife, parent, etc.) account.
   4. Type.
      a. Regular — no minimum balance, free checks.
      b. Deluxe — personalized checks, service charge for each check deducted from balance each month (10¢/check). $300 minimum balance.
B. Savings account
   1–3. Same as for a checking account.
   4. Social Security Number.
   5. Pays 5% a year interest.

(Kettering, 1975: 45)

(For a discussion of techniques of role-playing, see below.) The role-play should then be followed by a discussion session where the students may ask questions on matters that seem unclear to them. It is absolutely vital that the topic is relevant to the students' needs. The automobile exercise is of no use to students who have no intention of driving or buying a car, but it is one of our most successful exercises with those students who do. These exercises may be given as group or individual assignments depending on such factors as the length and complexity of the assignment, and the number of students in the class, etc. Some of Kettering's other exercises are on 'The supermarket', 'Telephone installation', 'Looking for an apartment', 'Hospital facilities', etc. These may not be typical of your students' needs, but they are of basic importance to our students, and these exercises serve their purpose very well. Simply look around you, think of what your students need to know, and then write out the questions for them to find out; that's all, and you have yourself a perfectly good community centered task.

Problem-solving activities

These exercises are just what they sound like; the students are presented with a problem and some alternative solutions from which they have to choose one. The following exercise, again from Kettering (1975: 54) contains directions for use as well:

A camping trip

You are going on a three-day camping trip up in the mountains. You will carry *everything* you need for the three days on your back. Since you are going into the mountains, it will be cold. This kind of trip is called a pack trip because you walk and carry everything you take with you on your back in a bag called a 'pack'. You have decided that you can't carry more than 25 pounds on your back comfortably. You made a list of things you want to take with you but they add up to more than 25 pounds. Now you have to read your list and include only the most important items. Remember they cannot add up to more than 25 pounds including the pack. Also remember that you will not see anyone for the three days and must include everything you need in order to survive.

You must come to a decision in your groups (and be sure you add up weights so they don't total more than 25 pounds). You must be able also to tell why you chose each item. There is no one correct list although certain items must be included on each list. When you have finished your list, choose a representative from your group to present your list to the other groups. You may challenge or be challenged by another group to tell why you chose an item so be sure you can justify each item.

If you don't understand the meaning of any item, you may ask your instructor.

List:

6 lb sleeping bag	3 lb extra pair of shoes
3 lb pack	6 lb water container (full of water)
1 lb pillow	4 lb camera
6 oz small book to record what you see	6 lb 3-day supply of food
8 oz swimming suit	12 oz plate, fork, knife, spoon
4 oz dish soap	12 oz insect repellant
4 oz tooth paste	2 lb extra set of clothing
2 oz tooth brush	3 lb fishing pole
1 lb pot to cook in	6 oz towel
1 lb flashlight	1 oz matches
1 lb rain jacket	

16 ounces = 1 pound; oz = ounce; lb = pound

I used this exercise when I taught in Sweden last fall, and it was my first successful effort at getting my students to talk freely. They protested at once that one should not go alone into the mountains, laughed aloud at the notion of a swimming suit, pointed out to me who had not thought of it that you don't need any insect repellent when it is cold in the mountains because then there are no insects. My quiet Swedes became positively talkative, and it illustrates a basic principle of these exercises; the closer you can come to the students' interests and prior experience, the more successful the exercise will be. Being Swedes, all of my students had been on camping trips, and they knew what they were talking about.

These exercises may seem to be ideal for developing communicative competence, but most of them are communicative performance exercises for developing linguistic competence and carry no socio-cultural information. The teacher can of course sum up the discussion with a comment on the relative acceptability in our culture of the various alternatives, but he should recognize that these activities tend to confirm the cultural bias of the students. I tried one activity called 'Dinner at an American home' in which as a guest you are served liver which you hate. What to do? Of the listed alternatives, the Swedes settled on the same rule I have: Eat it and pretend you like it. The Finn, however, said she would say nothing but not eat it, the Columbian said she would say her doctor had told her not to eat liver, and the German stated emphatically that she would tell the hostess that she didn't like liver. We had a nice discussion about cultural relativity, but I failed to convince them that it might be considered that in Sweden my rule was possibly a more viable alternative.

I prefer to hand these exercises out in class on the same day I intend to do them rather than have the students read them through at home. Although I waste time going through the problem, explaining words and such, the interest level of the group seems much higher when they can get at the problem immediately. Experiment with your classes and see which works best for you. If you are pressed for time, by all means have your students prepare at home.

Francine Shumann suggests an exercise which is a combination of the community oriented task and problem solving.[4] Give the students a suitable Ann Landers problem but with her answer removed, then send them out in the community to ask Americans what their suggested solution for the problem would be. The next time the class meets, they all compare notes and finally Landers' answer is read. There is a lot of cultural information in such an activity.

Most of the problem-solving activities involve group work, so you need to give thought to a few basic considerations. How large should a group be? Well, it depends partly on the size of your class, but here at Lackland I would not have more than four or five in a group. How will you group the students, the talkative ones in one group and the quiet ones in another, or all mixed up? Since expert opinion can be found in favor of every possible alternative, do as you like. I prefer a mixed bag, myself. Should the groups be fluid or permanent? It is a temptation to have permanent groups because it is convenient, lends itself to competition, and saves time. But members in a set group will quickly establish set patterns of relationships, the opposite of what you want in these activities where there should be as much talk as possible in reaching an agreement. Switch the groups around, and change the group leaders as well.

As a final remark on problem-solving activities, I'd like to qualify an earlier point. I said that the teacher should not correct, but you normally get a lot of peer teaching and correction in these activities, and that is as it should be. It will seem like correction to you, but actually the students only help when someone gets stuck or if they don't understand. The emphasis is on putting meaning across, not on linguistic forms.

Role-play

Role-plays are exercises where the student is assigned a fictitious role from which he has to improvise some kind of behavior towards the other role characters in the exercise. I am not considering the acting out of set dialogues or plays as role-play, nor the acting out of dialogues and plays written by the students themselves. In some role-plays, as the one on opening a bank account above, the student may simply be assigned the role of playing himself, but then you have a simulated situation rather than real role-play. The two basic requirements for role-play, as I see it, is improvization and fictitious roles.

Role-play can be very simple and the improvization highly controlled, or it can be very elaborate. It is primarily a matter of student proficiency which you should choose. Certainly role-play can be used in beginning classes.

The format of a role-play consists of three basic parts: the situation, the roles, and useful expressions. Occasionally a section on background knowledge is needed for advanced role-play. The *Situation* sets the scene and the plot, i.e. explains the situation and describes the task or action to be accomplished — again the task can be very simple, such as a telephone call, or very elaborate as settling a complex business deal. The situation is a good place to include specific cultural information if that is part of the objectives of a given role-play.

The *Roles* section assigns the roles, the list of characters. The roles should all have fictitious names; it aids the willing suspension of disbelief. Here you need to include such information as personality, experience, status, personal problems and desires, and the like. A role can be very simple, merely a skeleton name and status, or quite elaborate. But role descriptions should not be overly elaborate — unlike the situation, which may very well be — because then the playing of the role becomes a matter of clever acting and that is not the objective. On the contrary, it is inhibiting and counterproductive. You want the student himself to create the personality through hints of background or behavior like 'educated in a convent, strong moral views, . . .' about an applicant for a job as marriage counsellor or 'very particular, constantly mentions things she doesn't like' about a woman buying a house. I get a strong impression of their personalities from just those snippets of characterization.

In *Useful expressions* goes the linguistic information, primarily expressions, phrases, and technical vocabulary (an efficient way to teach vocabulary); but certainly grammar patterns which are necessary also fit in here, e.g. wh-questions for an interview situation. We try to incorporate as much sociolinguistic information as possible in this section. In a role-play about a car accident, the wife of one driver is angry with both the police and with the young boy who hit their car. It can be useful to know how to express anger with a policeman in an acceptable manner, and in this section we deliberately try to incorporate register and mood variation in language. And a word of caution when you write your own role-play; be careful not to have your men talk like women and vice versa. In a section on compliments, there was a sample expression 'What a lovely dress you are wearing' which was fine with me, but the male instructors rejected it out of hand as woman talk — they'd never say that. Language is much more marked for sex than we are consciously aware of.

Background knowledge is occasionally an essential section. It is no good at all to ask students to act out roles which demand a general knowledge they don't have. In order to act out a school board meeting on open classrooms, a town meeting on local industrial pollution, or a newspaper interview on the problem of the aged, the students must have subject matter information prior to the role-play. It need not be complicated at all, a short reading assignment, a lecture by the teacher or, always appreciated, a guest lecturer, a film, etc. But some source of knowledge is necessary, or the role-play won't come off.

But enough of talking about role-play; let's look at one. Here is a role-play by John Hoover (Paulston *et al.*, 1975), still in experimental stage:

Role playing: Buying a house

Situation:

Mr and Mrs Smythe are interested in buying a house in Pittsburgh, as Mr Smythe's company has transferred him from the San Francisco office. They are being shown a house in Shadyside by the real estate agent. The Smythes have three children aged 4, 12 and 14, two dogs and two cars. The house they are looking at is a four-bedroom home with a small yard and a single garage. Between them, the couple must decide whether they will buy the house or not.

Roles:

Mr Smythe   — very anxious to find a house because this is the tenth one he and his wife have looked at. He's desperate and willing to compensate for any deficiencies. He wants to buy this house.

Mrs Smythe   — very particular about what kind of house they buy. She does not want to buy this house and constantly mentions things she doesn't like about it.

Fred Fraudly   — real estate agent, very anxious to sell the house to the Smythes because he gets a big commission if he does. He refutes all of Mrs Smythe's complaints about the house and tries to convince the couple to buy it.

Useful expressions:

Mr Smythe (to his wife):   'There's nothing wrong with this house — let's take it.'
'I'm tired of looking.'
'Don't be so picky. We can fix that.'

Mrs Smythe (to agent):   'What's the matter with the .... ?'
'The .... is all wrong.'
'There's no ....'
'The .... is too ....'

Fraudly: 'You won't find a better deal anywhere.'
'There's a .... within walking distance.'
'We'll give you easy terms with only $.......... down.'

Topics for discussion:

1. Age of house and type of construction
2. Floor plan
3. Number and size of rooms
4. Yard area and landscaping
5. Neighborhood — facilities, transportation, shopping, etc.

Vocabulary:

basement	built-in-cabinets	storage area
attic	double garage	mortgage
closet	central heating and air conditioning	down payment

(Paulston *et al.*, 1975: 24)

We worried about whether there were enough vocabulary items and added some. Can you think of some to add? The role descriptions I think are very good, they give me a general strategy for the characters. You could add roles by having the children participate, and if you changed the number of bedrooms to three, you would add conflict because two boys would have to share a room. Conflict is highly desirous in role-play as it motivates the characters to talk. Change the age of the children to 10, 12 and 14, and the conflict grows sharper. But you get the idea of beginning with a general situation, and then continuing to tinker and play with it.

Once you have a role-play, what do you do with it? Well, the procedures vary somewhat from play to play but these are basic guidelines. Depending on the type and level of class, we do a role-play once a week or every other week. The role-play is handed out in the beginning of the week, the situation and the rest of the information is gone through and explained, and then roles are assigned. It doesn't work very well to ask for volunteers; no one wants to volunteer for nasty characters, and it wastes a lot of class time, so we tend just to assign roles. The students take home the role-play exercises, learn the useful expressions, and think about what they might say on their own. When they perform the role-play in class, they stand up and walk about and they are not allowed to have the written copy in their hands. Occasionally the teacher takes one of the roles to keep the play moving; this is useful especially in the beginning when the students learn to do role-plays.

In role-plays which contain only a few roles, it might seem like a good idea to have several groups do the role-play simultaneously as group work; but this doesn't work. I don't know why, but it seems that successful role-play requires an audience even if it is only the rest of the class.

If such work is treated as rehearsal, and the groups later perform for the whole class, it will work well enough for elementary role-plays which are strictly controlled with improvization at a minimum, as in this very simple exercise. After we had worked through a dialogue and drills on the grammar pattern, modals in polite requests, each pair of students was given a set of cards but each student saw only his own card. One card would say:

> You are in London on a business trip and you have Saturday free. You want to visit the British Museum but you don't know if it is open on Saturday. You also want to know how much the entrance fee is. Call up and find out.

The other card said:

> The British Museum is open Monday through Saturday, 9 a.m. to 5 p.m. There is no entrance fee.

The students then had to pretend to call up their partners and request whatever information the card instructed them to. (Each set was different.) The person who answered was not to give more information than he was asked for so he couldn't just read off his card. It may seem to you that this exercise is so simple it is not worth doing, but to a beginning class it is difficult and challenging enough. A role-play like this lends itself perfectly to be followed by an out-of-class community oriented task, where the students have to call up a native speaker in a real situation for some piece of information. It will have students practicing telephone dialogues with a vengeance — my students certainly did.

In some exercises, part of preparing for the role-play involves acquiring some background or technical knowledge, and it is an excellent way of co-ordinating lectures for aural listening comprehension or reading assignments with the rest of the class work. In preparing for this role-play in an advanced class, the students read an assignment on new ideas in education:

Role playing: A job interview

Situation:

Two elementary school teachers are applying for a teaching position in Langton School. One teacher is young, just out of college. The other is an older teacher with many years of experience. The principal, Harry Smith, interviews one teacher at a time (the other teacher leaves the room) in order to decide which one is best suited for the position. Each teacher tries very hard to convince the principal that he/she is the best one for the job.

After the principal has made a decision the class discusses his decision. How many agree with his choice? Disagree and why?

Cast of characters:

Miss Margaret Johnson — Young, just out of college; has completed all the required education courses along with practice teaching. — Is acquainted with all the new ideas

	in education and is eager to put ideas into practice. — Emphasizes her degrees and courses.
Mrs Cora Abernathy	— Older teacher; has taught elementary school for 20 years. — Loves children; is dedicated. — Emphasizes her experience.
The Principal	— Decides which teacher is best suited for the job.

Information that the principal should get from the two applicants:

I. Qualifications
    1. Education (college, refresher courses, in-training courses)
    2. Experience (number of years, city, kind of school)

II. Personal information (this information gives the principal a picture of the person, not just the worker)
    1. College graduation date
    2. Health
    3. Community activities
    4. Interests
    5. Marital status

III. References (the principal asks for the names of people he might contact who would be willing to vouch for the teacher's ability and character)
    Examples: a former principal
               a college professor

IV. Salary

V. Questions to help the principal determine if the applicant is suited for the job
    Examples: 'Do you like teaching?'
              'What are your feelings about the open classroom?'
              'What would you do if your class had a number of slow learners?'
              'How should children be punished for misbehavior?'
              'Do you believe in screaming at the children to get their attention?'
              'What are your feelings about homework?'
              'Why do you think you would be good for this job?'

(Paulston *et al.*, 1975: 44)

Such interviews may be made much more structured as in this other example from *Lifeline* by David Jones *et al.* (1973) where no prior reading is necessary.

A job interview

Interviewers:

You will have the applicant's application form in front of you, so look through it quickly and ask any further questions you think necessary on e.g. education, qualifications or previous experience. See which of the choices the applicant has marked, and find out whether this priority would have any effect on doing the job applied for. (Ask e.g. if the fact that the applicant did not mark 'the offered salary is attractive' means that he/she isn't interested in money at all! And so on.) Remember that you will only have a short time for the interview, so try and make all your questions to the point. Give hypothetical situations that might arise in the job, and ask what the applicant would do.

Interview for secretary/personal assistant

Apart from the basic requirements for the job, you must be satisfied that the applicant can work independently and be a genuine personal assistant. Question the applicants closely on previous jobs to check on this point; also see their reaction to hypothetical situations: e.g. 'what would you do if your boss had an important meeting the next day, but had left some vital papers in a town 100 miles away?' or 'what would you do if two important clients had by mistake been given the same time for appointments, and arrive at the same time?' Check on the question of travel at short notice.

Secretaries/personal assistants

i) *Barbara Arrowsmith.* 26 years old. Comprehensive school, good certificate in shorthand/typing from secretarial college. Several previous secretarial jobs, but only the last one involved a lot of real responsibility — as senior secretary in a small publishing company. Did French as part of her secretarial training but hasn't had occasion to use it for the last 5 years. Has only been abroad a few times, and the travel part of the job is a big attraction (although her fiancé is against her applying for the job just because of this aspect). Believes that the best technique in interviews is never to disagree with anything the interviewer says, and to be as polite and flattering as possible.

ii) *Gillian Henderson.* 28 years old. Grammar school, qualifications (A levels) in German, History and Economics. Secretarial skills self-taught, but has found them adequate so far in a variety of jobs — bank clerk, reporter for local paper, only secretary for underground newspaper (run by her ex-husband), courier for travel agency, researcher for author, unpaid assistant to organizer of a charity. Has lived abroad and speaks good German with some Finnish and Greek. Is used to taking responsibility and working independently, but has little idea of what would be involved in such a secretarial job. Believes that the best technique for interviews is to dominate as much as possible.

Howard Lagoze, an instructor in the Institute, developed a role-play in the format of a radio talk show, which required the students to listen to the radio at home. The teacher plays the commentator in order to keep up the pace, but with a fluent class that is not necessary. The students are assigned a variety of preposterous opinions on topics from death penalty to streaking, they prepare some kind of telephone call at home (not allowed to read from notes), and act it out the next time in class. The class I saw had a rollicking good time doing it, got good practice in arguing a point, and finished the role-play with a discussion on the social values of talk shows where the students contributed with observations on talk shows in their own country. There was a marked difference in the various cultural approaches of dealing with same phenomenon — a teaching point in itself.

An occasional procedural problem in role-plays is that one student will hog the show. When students are trained to do role-play, they should learn that whoever plays chairman, judge, commentator, principal, or whatever role who is in charge of the proceedings, has as his responsibility the task of keeping any one person from talking too much. It is an infrequent problem.

In some role-plays, not all players know the task or strategy of the other players, and the actual role-play is preceeded by 'secret' group work. Oxford University Press' (1973) *The Bellcrest Story* is of this order with many company board meetings and business deals. I'll finish by telling you about one that our students do, written by Dale Britton (in Paulston *et al.*, 1975: 51). It is a courtroom scene; some students have been charged with violations such as screaming and hollering in front of the university dormitory at 2.00 a.m., kicking dogs, or turning over park benches — all actual suits, by the way. Some students are counsel for the defense, others for the prosecution, and the rest are witnesses. They then go into group work planning their defense and prosecution, respectively, of their various cases, but no group knows what the others are planning. They get a lot of legal information, not at all useless for foreign students, in the process. The day I visited a class doing this role-play, the young man charged with screaming and hollering claimed in his defense that he had been attacked by two men, who tried to kidnap him while he was on his way home from the Computer Center, where he had been working, and that he had screamed for help. Subsequent witnesses brought out the fact that he was the son of wealthy parents and a man of staid and studious character. An eye-witness attested to having seen two men fleeing as the police officer approached to make the arrest. The witnesses were subjected to a very tough grilling by the counsel for the prosecution — incidentally a very shy Thai student who rarely spoke in class — but to no avail. The witnesses could not be shaken, and they improvised right along to meet the many questions, designed on the spot to trip them up. The judge's verdict of not guilty was greeted with cheers by the class.

I hope you get the same feeling I had in watching these students, that they were having great fun and that they were very pleased with themselves in being able to follow and handle unexpected arguments in a language they were far from fluent in. As they were struggling with the language in proper court procedure — they knew more about it than I did — they were also processing rules and beliefs of our judiciary system which are basic to our cultural values. I suppose you might say they were wasting time, they weren't studying grammar, or vocabulary or learning reading skills, but I would say that all the study of English skills is a waste of time if we don't also teach our students how to function in our culture with those skills.

Notes

1. To explain the chatty style of this chapter, I should mention that it was first delivered as a talk on the stage of Lackland auditorium. I am not sure I would dare do it today, but then I was young and foolhardy and on the stage behind me I had organized a 'class' of some twelve volunteer students from among Lackland's regular students, all dignified military men. The audience had handouts as did the students and whenever I came to the exercises discussed in the paper, I just turned around and did them on the stage with the students. Luckily it worked, and one of my more gratifying professional moments came when the Lackland audience confessed they would never had believed those activities were do-able with their students if they had not seen it with their own eyes. That was in the early days of communicative teaching!
2. That work was later published as Kettering (1975) and Paulston, Brunetti, Britton & Hoover (1975).
3. I probably didn't know it at the time, but this technique is known as Read and Look Up, developed by Michael West (1960) from a technique used by actors to memorize scripts.
4. Francine Schumann as cited in John H. Schumann (1974).

References

JOHNSON, F. C. 1970, personal communication from then Professor of English at the University of Papua and New Guinea, now at Kenda University, Japan.

JONES, D. *et al.*, 1973, *Lifeline*. Stockholm: Kursverksamheten vid Stockholms Universitet.

KETTERING, J. 1975, *Developing Communicative Competence: Interaction Activities in English as a Second Language*. Pittsburgh: The University Center for International Studies.

Oxford University Press, \1973, | *The Bellcrest Story*. London: Oxford University Press.

PAULSTON, C. B. 1974, Linguistic and communicative competence. *TESOL Quarterly* 8, 4, 347–62.

PAULSTON, C. B., BRUNETTI, B., BRITTON, D. and HOOVER, J. 1975, *Developing Communicative Competence: Roleplays in English as a Second Language*. Pittsburgh: University Center for International Studies.

RIVERS, W. 1972, Talking off the top of their heads. *TESOL Quarterly* 6, 1, 71–81.

—— 1973, From linguistic to communicative competence. *TESOL Quarterly* 7, 1, 25–34.

SCHUMANN, J. H. 1974, Communication techniques for intermediate and advanced/ ESL students. Paper presented at the TESOL convention, Denver, March 7.

WEST, M. 1960, *Teaching English in Difficult Circumstances* (pp. 12–13). London: Longmans, Green, and Company.

7 Comments on P. L. Hartman and E. L. Judd's *Sexism and TESOL Materials*[1]

What irritates and embarrasses me, as a scholar and a woman, about all this is the frequent tendency of feminists (female and male) to set up their framework and then stuff facts in willy-nilly, whether they fit or not. Nobody would make a mistake like 'the ambassador and his aide' when mid-page is listed 'Madam Ambassador' if the presumption weren't already there, simply waiting to be buttressed with data, accurate or no. It is a dishonest way of inquiry, and supports rather than discourages anti-feminism; hence my irritation. The notion of bias and discrimination in textbooks is an important one which deserves better than to be belittled by such careless work.

Another form of dishonesty in investigation is unrepresentative and biased sampling. For any quotation from Rutherford (1975) that might be interpreted as down-putting to women, it is easy to find one that puts down men; such passages are not mentioned. Actually, Rutherford is just being funny:

Ernie: We've always had a special arrangement; she (his wife) makes all the little decisions and I make all the big decisions.
Pete: How does it work out?
Ernie: Fine, except that no big thing has come up yet.
(Rutherford, 1968: 294).

This is not an MCP's remark on the social institution of marriage, but a joke which works exactly by pricking the male ego. I find it dishonest to portray Rutherford as a sexist who uses 'women as a class as the butt of jokes' (Hartman & Judd, 1978: 385). Everyone is the butt of Rutherford's jokes and to claim anything else is distorted scholarship. And please, how about a sense of humor?

Apart from the weaknesses of H & J's 'Sexism', and I won't continue with them, the article brings to light some issues in textbook writing which

70

deserve a constructive discussion, and we have been remiss in that aspect. Let me mention a few issues that we need to think about.

One must remember that, while writers may write for the love of it, commercial publishers publish for money, and that fact of life has implications for textbook writing. Often there may be a tension between, say, concern for large sales (surely also shared by the writer) and the writer's ideas of efficient language learning. I think for instance that highly topical or present political events are good topics for class discussion: students can be assigned to read the newspapers, American cultural reaction to events can be explained, etc. Nixon and Watergate was probably the most successful topic for the role-play 'The radio talk show' (Paulston *et al.*, 1975: 28), yet the published version has no mention of it. One learns not to overtly date material because a few years later that makes the materials seem hopelessly out of date.

I also believe that the more contextualized, functional, and personally relevant text material can be, the more the students care to learn from them. But I also realize that such concerns are in direct contrast to creating texts that have a general applicability to the largest possible audience. So one compromises. H & J mention without comment that *Roleplays* contains 26 characters whose sex cannot be determined. In their sexism-hunt, this did not interest them, but surely in a consideration of the division of labor between sexes, it merits some attention that an inordinately high number of characters lacks sexual identity. What happened in the writing of those materials was this: Men and women at times use different language and in working on the role-plays we paid a lot of attention to male and female speech, partially because we are linguists and it interested us, but mostly because we wanted to achieve as authentic language use as possible. But in trying out the materials, the teachers reported repeatedly that the students disliked playing a part of the other sex, and so in the interest of versality and practicality of the materials we threw out much of the sex-linked speech and 'uni-sexed' many of the characters, and so lost in detailed verisimilitude. But the gain was worth the loss, and I would make the same decision today. However, I would make one change. In looking over *Roleplays* again, I see to my chagrin that in spite of our care to use 'double-sexed' proper names like Pat, Chris and Terry which can equally well be taken to refer to men or women, the pronoun 'he' creeps in every so often and blows the game. These days I would settle for 's/he' (with a note to the teacher to discuss this usage), awkward as it is, because I think the gain in versatility is worth it.

What is not worth it, I think, is the de-sexing of cultural scenes. It is virtually impossible to write culture-free materials (science fiction is the closest) and certainly not desirable either. This leads straight to the dilemma whether one accurately portrays the culture or presents some kind of idealized version in conformance with one's ideology. H & J cite *English for Today* (Slager, Norris & Paulston, 1975) without much approval, which I find strange because no book can have been more carefully watched for sexism, implied or otherwise. Too carefully watched, I think. The first edition had a chapter set on an Ohio farm where the mother was in her kitchen cooking, the father in the fields plowing with the big tractor, etc. Just rural America. But, no, it was clearly sexist stereotyping, and so in the second edition out went Mom's kitchen and in came a *person-kitchen* or the family's kitchen or something equally silly, and by the time the reading was all desexed, the Ohio farm was like no farm in the Midwest I have ever known. I can understand that a feminist objects to the sex roles on a Midwest farm, and you won't find me living there, but that does not grant me the license to falsify a cultural phenomenon. That chapter is a thorn in my flesh and I won't do it again; I think it was intellectually dishonest in the interest of a publisher's expediency. (It was the result of official McGraw-Hill policy.)

Finally, the last issue that I would like to bring up concerns the problem in material writing of having the text meet the specific demands of its genre. For instance, in a dialogue you have to have people speak, and that means a style of spoken English the way live people talk and not of the 'I am pleased to meet you/Are you pleased to meet me?/I am not pleased to meet you' variety (Samelson, 1974: 7). Natural sounding dialogues are remarkably difficult to achieve.

In role-plays, if they are to 'work' in a classroom, if they are to generate some excitement in the playing, there must be some sort of conflict to be resolved. One of the easiest ways to achieve such conflict is to make the characters rather disagreeable. When *Roleplays* went to press, the typesetter (an ardent feminist) refused to set the manuscript because of its sexist portrayal of women as unpleasant creatures, she claimed. So I had to go through all the male roles and list their characteristics to show her that the males were, if anything, even worse than the females. She consented to set the manuscript, but clearly she didn't think much of what she held to be our worldview. However, she was quite wrong in this her interpretation, for the disagreeable people in *Roleplays* are not our commentary on *la condition humaine* but a requirement of the genre. Similarly, Rutherford's put-downs are an expedient way of achieving humor in dialogues, a very difficult trick, as a myriad of dull dialogues bears witness to.

I bring up the issue about genre requirements because material writers need to be conscious of them. It is much easier than one might think to be selectively critical, condescending or ironic, and always pick on women or salesmen or squareheaded Swedes without really meaning to. In such a situation not only H & J, but all of us, would have cause for complaint.

I have mentioned three problem areas in materials writing as they relate to the portrayal of women and women's role in society, which readily came to my mind. A systematic analysis of requirements and decisions that must be met during the process of designing and writing materials would of course turn up more such problem areas. My purpose with these comments has not been to be exhaustive; rather I wanted to indicate the need for the direction of a critically positive approach with which we can deal with the problems of sexism in materials. Social discrimination in any form is abhorrent, nonetheless so if it is done unwittingly. The matter deserves serious attention rather than a trivial treatment which recommends 'equal quantity of sex-linked referents' and the avoidance of words like 'mankind' (Hartman & Judd, 1978: 392). Such attention needs neither feminism or machismo but shared humanism (and I, for one, refuse words like 'hupersonism'). We do need to sort through the problems and help each other: No man is an island, entire of itself.

Notes

1. I have here deleted the specific criticism of a profeminist article and only include the general comments with which the article concluded.

References

HARTMAN, P. L. and JUDD, E. L. 1978, Sexism and TESOL materials. *TESOL Quarterly* 12, 4 (December).

PAULSTON, C. B., BRITTON, D., BRUNETTI, B. and HOOVER, J. 1975, *Developing Communicative Competence: Roleplays in English as a Second Language.* Pittsburgh: University Center for International Studies, University of Pittsburgh.

RUTHERFORD, W. 1968, *Modern English,* 1st edn. Harcourt, Brace & World, Inc.

—— 1975, *Modern English,* 2nd edn. New York: Harcourt, Brace & Jovanovich.

SAMELSON, W. 1974, *English as a Second Language, Phase One.* Reston, Va.: Reston Publishing Co.

SLAGER, W., NORRIS, W. and PAULSTON, C. B. 1975, *English Today,* Book IV. New York: McGraw-Hill.

8 Notional Syllabuses Revisited: Some Comments[1]

There is little new under the sun in language teaching. Saint Augustine developed a dialogue method of teaching and Cicero advocated a form of controlled composition. John Florio's (1578) *First Fruits* contains passages on social calls, courting, quarrelling and the like, and Kelly (1969: 121) cites Erasmus on the 'well-turned insult', all in a notional approach to language teaching. What does change is the constellation of classroom techniques into various methods and, of course, theories which attempt to account for these methods. On either count, Wilkins' (1976, 1981) work lies outside such concerns; he does not deal with methods of language teaching nor with any theory of language acquisition.

What Wilkins does[2] is to advocate an approach to syllabus design which specifies the content and the teaching points according to the criteria of notions and functions. (Meaning and function of language is seen as more important than form of language.) Now, one chooses criteria in scholarly work either on theoretical grounds or on empirical, i.e. on experience and common sense. NSR very much does the latter. Wilkins' approach is quite atheoretical; it says nothing about how languages are learned, either neurologically, psychologically or socially, and what this means in effect is that the generalizability of this approach is limited. Wilkins is very clear about the limitations; he is talking about Indo-European languages and cultures (1981: 3). I read that to mean European; surely one cannot talk in any meaningful way of Indo-European cultures. The needs of the language students in western Europe are very much those that Wilkins outlines; they need to focus on expressing the meaning and content of those language forms most of them have studied for several years, but without acquiring the ability to negotiate meaning in the target language.

The needs of these students are very different from the needs of our Japanese or Latin American students who have never studied English and now find themselves living in an English-speaking community. They need to learn not a number of finite speech acts, but rather structures which will do them for a number of functions: Widdowson's (1971) instruction, invitation, advice and prayer all expressed through the imperative form.[3] My basic objection to an exclusively notional approach is just this; language forms are generative while notions are not, and since one cannot in fact divorce function from form in language, it makes more sense to me to organize a syllabus along linguistic forms which can generate infinite meanings and many functions, rather than to organize the content along a finite list of functions.

But that is my preference and that is how I learn languages, and if we know anything about language learning by now, it is that learners differ. For all I know, Wilkins is musically talented with a good eye for shape and form — and that is not quite as silly a comment as it sounds. I am suggesting that it is possible that right hemisphere dominant learners may prefer a functional organization of language material while left hemisphere dominant learners prefer a formal organization. Whatever the explanation for learner preference, the conclusion is obvious: language learning materials should incorporate both a formal and a functional axis.

My other reservation about the NSR approach is that it is exclusively concerned with the target language, and so all the cross-cultural concerns of communicative competence oriented approaches simply disappear. Wilkins mentions complaints. Teaching official, conventional complaints to a Japanese is not at all the same thing as teaching complaints to, say, our Latin American students. The latter have rules in Spanish which strike me, having heard many of their complaints, as similar to American rules. But the Japanese do not complain in Japanese,[4] so the very speech act has to be learned as well as its linguistic coding. The point I am making is that even if you take a notional approach to syllabus design, any speech act will still have both formal coding as well as functional rules for appropriate usage, and if NSR attempts to deal with this issue, I missed it. To teach our students 16 ways of asking permission to borrow the telephone (NS: 60–61; which presumably Wilkins also would think excessive) would be remiss without also teaching them when and where they could do so.

But that is only one side of the problem. In spite of the very general guidelines our students receive for the speech act of asking permission, it has never happened that a student has come into my office and asked permission to borrow my phone, and I think that I cannot honestly attribute this to the detailed excellence of our teaching. Rather, there are communicative competence universals which pertain to speech acts, and around the world, students know about super/subordinate relationships, about teacher/student relationships, with the result that no student will ask to borrow my telephone because it would be inappropriate wherever one finds telephones. No doubt some reader will now write me with a counter example, but I hope the point I have made is clear; there are universals for the social use of speech acts, and in this case what the student needs are linguistic forms he himself can generate to clothe his communicative intent. Intent of speech acts transfers from one language to another without difficulty for the student, and it is only when the intent is inappropriate in the target culture that the student gets into trouble.

I agree with Wilkins that in order to learn a language students must use it communicatively if they are to reach any degree of fluency. Clearly the curriculum (syllabus) must be so organized that it structures students' activities into communication, but I see no valid argument for eliminating a formal linguistic axis for the organization of language content.

Apart from these objections, I would like to make clear that I think the issues Wilkins raises well merit concern by anyone who is interested in syllabus design. These issues need to become incorporated into a theory of language acquisition or at least stated in terms of testable hypotheses, and either established or dismissed. Empirical criteria should be established by facts, not on logico-deductive reasoning for or against.

Notes

1. In the 1981 Spring issue of the then very new journal *Applied Linguistics* in the Discussion Section, D. A. Wilkins had a piece on 'Notional Syllabuses Revisited'. H. Widdowson, editor, asked C. Brumfit and me for some brief reactions to that article, and this chapter is what I wrote.
2. I should say that I don't see much difference between *Notional Syllabuses* (NS) (Wilkins, 1976) and 'Notional Syllabuses Revisited' (NSR) (Wilkins, 1981); key concepts have not changed, and Wilkins says as much, 'general orientation and philosophy of syllabus design has not changed' (p. 10).
3. 'Bake the pie in a slow oven', 'Come for dinner tomorrow,' 'Take up his offer,' 'Forgive us our trespasses' (Widdowson, 1971: 38–9).
4. Of course, Japanese grouse as the rest of us, but they would not, for instance, return damaged merchandise to a department store with complaints of shoddy goods as certainly an American would. Over the years, I have heard many complaints from our students in the English Language Institute but never from a Japanese. And we even teach complaints.

References

FLORIO, J. 1578, *Florio his Firste Fruites*. Reprint by Arundell del Re, Formosa, 1936.
KELLY L. G. 1969, *25 Centuries of Language Teaching*. Rowley, Mass.: Newbury House.
WIDDOWSON, H. G. 1971, The teaching of rhetoric to students of science and technology. In *Science and Technology in a Second Language*. London: Center for Information on Language Teaching and Research.
WILKINS, D. A. 1976, *Notional Syllabuses*. Oxford: Oxford University Press.
—— 1981, Notional Syllabuses Revisited. *Applied Linguistics* 2, 1.

9 Applied Linguistics: The Use of Linguistics in ESL

An exhaustive bibliography on the topic of this paper would fill pages, for linguists have written extensively on the subject. They have also disagreed extensively, from Newmark's (1970)

> the transformationist's analysis of verb phrase constructions, beginning with Chomsky's simple C(M) (have+en) (be+ing) V formula, brings startling simplicity and clarity to our understanding of the grammatical structure of a number of discontinuous and elliptical verb constructions; transformational grammar seems to offer suggestions neatly and precisely for what a program teaching English verb structure would have to include. (Newmark 1970: 213)

to Chomsky's (1966) own

> frankly, I am rather sceptical about the significance, for the teaching of languages, of such insights and understanding as have been attained in linguistics or psychology. (Chomsky, 1966: 43)

and he adds later

> It is the language teacher himself who must validate or refute any specific proposal. (Chomsky, 1966: 45)

Who is right? In a sense, that is what this paper is about.

If by applied linguistics, we mean the use linguists put their knowledge to in order to get things done in the real world, it is immediately clear that applied linguistics means a lot more than merely language teaching (Corder, 1975; Roulet, 1975; Spolsky, 1978). It is generally recognized that translation is one aspect of applied linguistics but in this context less frequently pointed out that translation existed centuries before linguistics, and, in fact, provided a powerful impetus for the development of the discipline of linguistics in the United States. Missionaries, in groups like the Wycliffe Bible Translators and the Summer Institute of Linguistics, were dedicated to spreading the Word of God by translating the gospels into primarily unwritten languages. They found that they made awkward mistakes. To give but one example: many languages have inclusive *we* ('all of us guys') and exclusive *we* ('my friend and I but not you guys'), and if you have never run into them before, the inclusive/exclusive feature of the first person plural pronoun is far from immediately apparent. So it is not surprising that the missionaries inadvertently translated 'Our Father' with exclusive *we,* and subsequently discovered to their horror the Aymara Indians' interpretation of a God for white folk only, which notion was the last on earth they had intended. Accordingly, scholars like Kenneth Pike (1947) of the Summer Institute of Linguistics in his *Phonemics: A Technique for Reducing Languages to Writing,* Eugene Nida (1949) of the American Bible Society in his *Morphology: The Descriptive Analysis of Words,* and later H. A. Gleason (1955) of the Hartford Seminary Foundation in *An Introduction to Descriptive Linguistics* were genuinely concerned with what came to be known as 'discovery procedures', the analysis of unknown and unwritten languages.

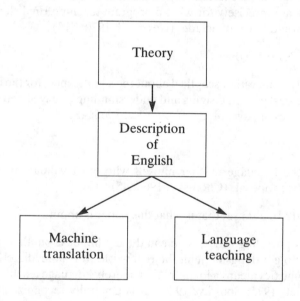

Source: Roulet, 1975: 71

FIGURE 9.1

One result of the practical bent of anthropologists and missionaries was that it inadvertently developed techniques for language learning through the focus on discovery procedures, such as substitution drills. Partially, I suspect, the audio-lingual method, also known, albeit erroneously, as the linguistic method, was a historical accident, created in wartime by linguists who turned to their established procedures for getting things done. The point I am making here is that there is very much a two-way street between theory and application, between translation and linguistics and language learning and that problems in the real world do touch and test the development of theory. Linguistics as we know it today would never have existed if people had not tried to do things with language, all the way back to Pāṇini. We clearly have to reject a model like that in Figure 9.1 as inaccurate and misleading, where the direction of influence is in one direction only.

There are two ways of answering the question of the significance of linguistics for language teaching. One is to argue from theory to speculative claims in a logico-deductive manner as Newmark does. The evidence for his 'startling simplicity and clarity' claim is his own expert opinion. This is by far the most common approach, and the literature is replete with grand claims of what linguistics can achieve for the language learner. Furthermore, these claims cannot be dismissed on the grounds that there is no evidence to support them for they are made by men of stature and experience with language teaching, like Fries (1945), Lado (1957), Moulton (1970) and Allen & Corder (1975) to pick three classics and one more recent work.

The other way is of course to argue from data and to document the use of linguistic insights and knowledge in the classroom. We could ask the teachers of ESL what they find helpful from their training in linguistics and what they actually use in the classroom. Such data will share the weakness of all self-report data and should therefore be augmented by actual classroom observation, where the observer especially watches for any evidence of the use of linguistic knowledge. One can examine syllabi and textbooks for similar evidence as well as consider the claims in recent journal articles with a practical bent; the latter also a type of self-report data. One might consider examining the content of teacher training courses, but on second thought I think one will find merely that the director considered such content important but not whether the teachers in fact would ever use such knowledge.

I have attempted a rather cursory investigation of this kind. Our English Language Institute, modelled after the Michigan ELI, teaches English to some 200 students with some 25 instructors (the exact figures vary from term to term). Sixteen instructors returned questionnaire responses in which they (most of them are Teaching Assistants (TAs) in the Department of Linguistics) were asked to rate their course work on a scale 1–10 in usefulness for teaching purposes. I interviewed seven TAs who were students in a supervision seminar. I observed classes and immediately found an interesting research problem.

In none of the three grammar classes I observed was there any indication that the instructors had any linguistics training beyond a good public schools ninth grade class with Warriner (1973; now Warriner, Whitten & Griffith, 1975), any overt, clear, solid, unmistakeable evidence that the teacher was a linguist in the making. I confess that this fact surprised me. One of the instructors was a young man in the throes of his doctoral linguistic comprehensive exams, which is possibly the period in one's life of the most intense consciousness of matters linguistic. In an in-depth interview following my observation of his class, he made the following points:

1. He didn't use technical linguistics terms in the classroom (beyond 'indirect/ direct object focus in active/passive transformation') for the simple reason that the students would not understand it. (This attitude permeates the instructors' thinking in general.)
2. He found his knowledge of syntax very useful in selecting teaching points, i.e. what to teach and what to ignore about the passive construction as well as setting up and presenting the construction in model sentences on the board and in the explanations.
3. He thought the textbook exercises awful and that the best approach to teaching the passive is not through transformations of formal aspects of the active voice.

In essence, what we have here are cognitive and attitudinal influences of linguistics on the instructor which are not observable but nevertheless of extreme importance. It is a situation similar to documenting avoidance behavior in sociolinguistics, a very difficult problem. To compound the difficulty, we have an aspect of Labov's 'observer's paradox'. The young man had previously been admonished to beware of too much teacher talk by his regular supervisor, and we cannot exclude the possibility that he monitored carefully any linguistics jargon in my presence. Participant-observation is not a sufficient approach to data collection in problem areas which are so cognitively oriented as linguistics and teaching.

A third point should be made. It is surprising after 12 years of classroom observation in the ELI that I should be surprised. I take linguistics for granted and have just never looked for it, so to speak. The lack of its manifest presence,[1] when I was specifically looking, surprised me. This fact suggests a third way for answering our question about the significance of linguistics for language teaching, namely putting the two approaches together and using theory to guide our looking for supporting data, a common enough approach in experimental research. The model I propose using is that of Roulet's (1975), reproduced in Figure 9.2.

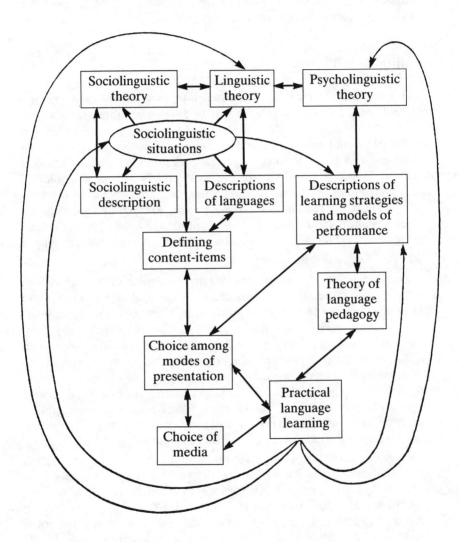

Source: Roulet, 1975: 83

FIGURE 9.2

His major point, which others (Spolsky, 1969) have made before him, is that various fields besides theoretical linguistics contribute to language teaching and that one needs to understand the processes of their inter-relationship as well. I propose to use Roulet's categories as a checklist for examining the possible contributions to language teaching we might find from linguistics in this broad sense of the word and then look for evidence that they occur somewhere in the teaching process.

Sociolinguistic Theory

This topic might usefully be divided into sociology of language and sociolinguistics. The sociology of language deals with language problems and language treatments at the national level as problems arise within and between ethnic and national groups in contact and competition. Choice of national language and of writing system, language standardization, bilingual education, language maintenance and shift efforts are all examples of language problems. Naturally ESL is affected by the choice of teaching Nigerian children to read in English, in choosing to teach Chicano children to read in Spanish and in English, but it is more at a level of global under-standing of contextual means and constraints than at a direct classroom level of application.

Sociolinguistics refers to an approach to description of language which takes into account the social features of a far from ideal hearer/speaker and seeks to account for the rules of linguistic variability, be it social, regional, cultural, gender, register or stylistic variation. (Labov has made the claim that the term 'sociolinguistics' is tautological since all linguistics need to do this.) Sociolinguistics is probably the area which has most influenced lan-guage teaching developments within the last ten years, especially through its work with sociolinguistic description on speech acts, pragmatics, discourse analysis and cross-cultural communication. There is no one sociolinguistic theory, and sociolinguists use notions and concepts from several disciplines, primarily from anthropology, linguistics and sociology. The work of Hymes, Labov and Bernstein may serve as representative examples. Hymes' notion of 'communicative competence' which draws on key concepts in ethno-graphy has more than any other theoretical model influenced a new direc-tion in language teaching (see below). Labov's (1969) work on Black English helped legitimize this dialect with formal descriptions of its rule-governed behavior and dispel ideas of sloppy, lazy speech. The interest in SESD (Standard English as a Second Dialect), as this special interest group is known in TESOL, and the many resultant publications (Baratz & Shuy,

1969; Dillard, 1972; Shuy & Fasold, 1970; Feigenbaum, 1970; Kochman, 1972; Mitchell-Kernan, 1971; Wolfram, 1969; Wolfram & Clarke, 1971) peaked in the late 1960s and early 1970s and at present form a less viable part of ESL. But the interest is bound to return because the basic problems are still with us, and as the basic groundwork was done in sociolinguistics, I am reasonably certain (I speak as a former SESD chairman) that ESL, or TESOL rather, will continue to be its spiritual and organizational home, an example of applied linguistics at its very best.

The attempts to explain, at a theoretical level, the educational failure of lower-class and minority children have been many and varied from Jensen's (1969) genetic model through cultural deprivation (Bereiter & Engelmann, 1966) to cultural differences (Abrahams & Troike, 1972; Burger, 1971; Cazden, John & Hymes, 1972; Saville-Troike, 1976; Spolsky, 1972; Trueba & Barnett-Migrahi, 1979). Much of the linguistic work on Black English was motivated exactly by the linguistic ignorance of the psychologists who wrote about the language of black children. Another series of theory building which has marginally found its way into ESL but nevertheless has much influenced the thinking of sociolinguists is that of the British sociologist Basil Bernstein (1971, 1972, 1973). He posits the notions of restricted and elaborated code of which the latter is crucial for school success. Working-class children through their socialization in position oriented families have limited access to an elaborated code and so do poorly in school. This is an enormous simplification of his very elaborate argument but is nevertheless the gist of the matter. Bernstein has been widely misunderstood in the United States[2] where his work has been totally inappropriately applied to Black children.

We see then that the use of sociolinguistic theory tends to be problem oriented in its applications, frequently dealing with the language learning difficulties children from other than mainstream groups experience in our schools.

Sociolinguistic situations

Sociolinguistic situations refer to the real world situation in which the students are going to use their English and so brings up the question of defining the objectives of language teaching in terms of the functions of these needs. 'English for Special Purposes' and 'English for Science and Technology' have been a major development during the last decade in ESL (Lackstrom, Selinker & Trimble, 1970; Richards, 1976; Selinker, Trimble & Vroman, 1972).

Sociolinguistic Description

This is the area where I think the most interesting work has been done in ESL during the last ten years, but then that may be a biased opinion. Still, my guess is that 20 years from now, when the Silent Way and Suggestopedia are gone, we will still use the sociolinguistic descriptions of speech acts, discourse, and cross-cultural communication which now surface in our journals.

Dell Hymes (1972a, 1972c, 1974), the anthropological linguist, has suggested that linguistic competence is not sufficient for an adequate description of language which must also take into account when, how and to whom it is appropriate to speak, that is a 'communicative competence' or in Grimshaw's (1973: 109) terms 'the systemic sets of social interactional rules'. More than any other single concept, the notion of communicative competence has influenced our thinking about teaching ESL. There are two major approaches within ESL at present, and one of them is a communicative approach to language teaching (Brumfit & Johnson, 1979; Canale & Swain, 1979; Candlin, 1975; Munby, 1978; Roulet & Holec, 1976; Widdowson, 1978; Wilkins, 1976). Such an approach argues that the focus of language teaching should be on language use rather than form, although most scholars consider linguistic competence to be part of communicative competence. The discrete units or teaching points of a lesson, syllabus, or textbook then cease being grammatical patterns, sequenced in an orderly manner, and instead become speech acts[3] or in Wilkins' terms notions and functions. Not that there is total agreement on this manner of organizing textbooks; in one of the latest issues of *Applied Linguistics* (1981, II, 1), both Brumfit and I argue against a purely functional approach in syllabus construction where the main argument is, I think, that language forms are generative while functions are not. One can, of course (and I would add should), combine form and function in one's teaching.

Johnson & Morrow's (1978) *Communicate* and (1979) *Approaches* were some of the first textbooks to adhere to a functional approach. Today it is a publisher's darling. A number of journal articles tackle the problem of speech act description (Borkin & Reinhart, 1978; Carrell & Konneker, 1981; Ervin-Tripp, 1976; Levinson, 1980; Rintell, 1979; Scarcella, 1979; Walters, 1979; Wolfson, 1981).

And interestingly enough sociolinguistics rated very high, right up with phonetics, on the questionnaire the ELI instructors had been asked to answer about the usefulness of linguistics for language teaching. All of them singled out speech act theory especially as helpful. I think this somewhat, to me at least, surprising response reflects the fact that although our cultural rules and ways of doing things permeate our life, we are rarely aware of those rules until they are broken. It is difficult to talk about and teach cultural rules without any training. Several instructors commented that such study had given them a way of systematically organizing the data and a metalanguage — which they avoided using in the classroom — to think about such phenomena. One instructor added that such understanding also allowed her to know exactly what questions to ask in the classroom in order to bring out a kind of cultural contrastive analysis of speech acts. A compliment in Japanese is not necessarily one in English (Wolfson, 1981), and students need to be made aware of that.

Finally, ESL teachers are sensitive to their students as human beings. In the words of one instructor: 'Sociolinguistics has helped me become aware of different cultural norms and *possible* differences, perhaps more importantly . . . It helps in dealing with the students on a personal level.'

Linguistic Theory and Descriptions of Languages

Back in 1969, Wardhough wrote a TESOL State of the Art paper in which he outlined the tenets of transformational-generative (TG) grammar and commented on the insights into language it gave. He concluded: 'However, neither the grammar nor existing descriptions give teachers any way of teaching these insights nor do they provide any way of assigning a truth value to the insights on an absolute scale, apparent claims to the contrary notwithstanding' (Wardhough, 1969: 12). I think Wardhaugh's remark still stands. The most intelligent statement of the value of TG grammar for language teaching was Robin Lakoff's (1969) 'Transformational grammar and language teaching' and she has since (Lakoff, 1974) retracted her words, saying she was simply mistaken. Rutherford's (1968) *Modern English,* for which claims were made that it followed a TG approach, in its second edition reflects a change toward more traditional grammar. In fact, we tend to find the same absence of overt linguistics in textbooks as I found in classroom observation. Furey (1972) found in an analysis of the grammatical rules and explanations very little difference in textbooks of respectively audio-lingual, direct method, TG grammar and eclectic orientation. Presumably this is so, she says, because of the pedagogical necessity of simplifications of rules.

There are of course linguistic theories other than TG grammar, such as case grammar (Nilsen, 1971) and tagmemics (Paulston, 1970) which are used for ESL purposes. The trouble is that few ESL teachers today are trained in structural linguistics, which I maintain is much more suitable for pedagogical purposes. In fact, what happens is that the eclectic approach exemplified by Quirk & Greenbaum (1973) (and Quirk, Greenbaum, Leech & Svartvik, 1972) is the generally prevailing approach in language teaching.

My view that theoretical linguistics has lacked any influence on language teaching during the last decade needs to be modified. Chomsky undeniably changed the climate of linguistic thought in the United States. Chomsky's attack of language acquisition as habit formation has had enormous consequences on our thinking about language teaching. Language learning as a creative act is the basic foundation of most present-day ESL methods and one source for our interest in error analysis.

The way teachers deal with errors in the classroom is closely influenced by their linguistic knowledge. Experienced teachers tend to correct what they judge to be performance errors with a reference to the rule and so elicit the correction from the student himself while a competence error repeated by several students will bring on a modelling by the teacher of the grammatical pattern, sometimes in a contrast to other familiar patterns, and a grammatical explanation of its function. I saw this repeated several times in my class observations. Thinking on one's feet and being able to come up with good example sentences is in fact what one instructor cites as the major benefit of her syntax course. Most instructors agree that syntax, standard theory, is too abstract to be of much use in the classroom but they cite the insight into *patterns* of English, into knowing what is rule-governed behavior and what needs to be memorized, into what structures are similar and different, into knowing what goes together as very useful in their teaching. One of them writes: 'Since I've studied linguistics I've become *more* convinced of the notion that language has a definite structure/system, which means I now no longer feel quite so helpless about teaching grammar.' The last point is important. It became very clear in the interviews that teachers dislike intensely to feel ignorant or uncertain about what they are teaching and that they worry about their explanations and presentation of teaching points. The study of linguistics brings them confidence and security, and they are very conscious about that relationship.

The instructors are unanimous in their opinion that phonetics is most useful; it is the only coursework that ranks higher than sociolinguistics. The reason is simple: 'I understand how the sounds are articulated and can tell the students'. It also develops their ear so they can hear and know what the students do wrong. It is hardly a recent development in linguistics; classic articulatory Eliza Doolittle period. They find basic concepts in phonemics useful but most reject generative phonology. Surprisingly, many also reject grammatical analysis, morphology, and field methods and less surprisingly, historical linguistics and Montague grammar. They all consider linguistic structures of English, in which they use Quirk & Greenbaum (1973), as basically boring but nevertheless essential.

We see then that even if I have doubt about the usefulness of present day linguistics for language teaching, our students do not. Even if they consider only two courses in linguistic theory — phonetics and English grammar — as core courses, they insist that the study of syntax brings them a *Weltanschaung,* a worldview of language which they find eminently useful.

Defining content items

By this term, Roulet means the selection and sequencing of language materials for the curriculum or textbook. Structural linguists gave a lot of thought and energy to the optimum selection and sequencing of language items, but these days this is an unfashionable topic. The occasional argument is rather whether one should teach function before form, and of course there is the notional-functional argument that syllabi should be organized on the basis of communicative functions rather than on grammatical patterns. As Canale & Swain (1979: 58) point out, there are no empirical data on the relative effectiveness or ineffectiveness of either approach.

Psycholinguistic Theory

In 1969 Wardhaugh predicted that cognitive psychology would influence language teaching for many years to come and thus far his prediction holds. Ausubel (1968) is still frequently cited in footnotes, everyone insists language learning must be meaningful, the notion of language learning as habit formation is dismissed, and there seems to be a general consensus that grammatical rules and explanations are beneficial for adults.[4]

Besides cognitive psychology, psycholinguistics (Clark & Clark, 1977; Dato, 1975; Taylor, 1976; Slobin, 1971) and neurolinguistics (Albert & Obler, 1978; Lenneberg & Lenneberg, 1975; Rieber, 1976) are topics of recent interest. Especially in regard to neurolinguistics, caution is needed in drawing implications for the classroom. At this point I think it is safe to say that the evidence (from aphasia, split brain operations, dichotic listening tests, etc.) indicates that individuals have different ways of learning for which there may be a biological foundation. But that was known before. I find the readings in neurolinguistics the most interesting in the language-learning field today. But I worry about premature applications, and I react against the fads which claim to draw on neurolinguistics.

In psycholinguistics, there has been much L2 acquisition research during the last decade. Douglas Brown, in an editorial in *Language Learning* in 1974, comments on the 'new wave' of research: 'for perhaps the first time in history, L2 research is characterized by a rigorous empirical approach coupled with cautious rationalism' (D. Brown, 1974: v–vi) and goes on to claim that 'the results of current L2 research will indeed have a great impact on shaping a new method' (D. Brown, 1974: v–vi). This hasn't happened, and it is still too early to see what the implications will be.

It is difficult to single out any specific studies, but the best place to begin is probably with Roger Brown's (1973) *A First Language*. Along with his basic finding that 'there is an approximately invariant order to acquisition for the 14 morphemes we have studied, and behind this invariance lies not modeling frequency but semantic and grammatical complexity (R. Brown, 1973: 379) (a finding supported by the L2 studies), he also carefully investigates the psychological reality of TG transformational rules, a notion he is forced to reject as invalid. Instead he posits the concept of semantic saliency, a notion which may hold direct implications for language teaching.

Whatever the implications for language teaching which we will eventually draw from this 'new wave' of L2 acquisition research, Brown is right in pointing out a major significance, the turning to empirical evidence rather than unsubstantiated claims and counterclaims.

The greatest surprise of the questionnaire response was to be found in the TAs' reaction to psycholinguistic theory. They held it of marginal utility. I will quote one instructor at length.

> Nothing very directly applicable; but by increasing my knowledge of the mental processes involved in language use (well, at least of people's theories about them), it's increased my . . . my what? I think this is a case where I have to resort to a general 'the more I know about language and language learning, the better teacher I'll be'. The most pertinent research (in reading, L1 acquisition, etc.) seems better at pointing out what variables are probably insignificant than at telling us which ones are important.

I think this attitude reflects the fact that we really don't know how people learn language.

Descriptions of Learning Strategies and Models of Performance

Theory of language pedagogy

A thorough exploration of these two topics would require a book or two to complete and take us too far afield for the purposes of this paper. The audiolingual method drew heavily on linguistics in its development. Today that method has been discredited, maybe at times unfairly, as it is blamed for infelicities which Fries certainly never intended. A careful reading of his *Teaching and Learning English as a Foreign Language* (Fries, 1945) will reveal it as sensible a book today as the day it was written.

In today's thinking about language teaching, psychology seems to play a larger part than linguistics. Cognitive code (John Carroll's term) is recognized as a general trend, with its emphasis on meaningful learning and careful analysis of linguistic structures. The congitive code approach can be considered a reaction against the audio-lingual, both from theoretical and practical viewpoints. The approach closely reflects the transformational-generative linguistic school of thought about the nature of language, and it is influenced by cognitive psychologists, critical of stimulus-reinforcement theory, such as Ausubel (1968). It holds that language is a rule-governed creative system of a universal nature. Language learning must be meaning-ful, rote-learning should be avoided, and the primary emphasis is on analysis and developing competence in Chomsky's sense of the word. We see the same nice fit between linguistic theory and psychological theory in cognitive code methodology as we once had in the audio-lingual method. The trouble with cognitive code is that I know of not one single textbook for beginning students which can be classified as strict cognitive code.

In practical fact, most language teaching specialists are eclectic and so are the textbooks they write. Carroll (1971) holds that there is nothing mutually exclusive in the theories of Skinner and of Lenneberg-Chomsky about language learning but rather that these theories are complementary. This opinion is reflected in the eclectic approach to methodology which is characteristic of most of the methods texts at the technique level. Most of the writers of these texts agree that all four skills — listening, speaking, reading and writing — should be introduced simultaneuosly, without undue post-ponement of any one. The importance of writing as a service activity for the other skills is generally recognized and there is considerable interest in con-trolled composition. No one talks any longer about memorizing long dialogues. Listening comprehension is still poorly understood on a theo-retical level, but there is more emphasis on the teaching of that skill. The crucial importance of vocabulary, the ignoring of which was one of the worst faults of the audio-lingual approach, is increasingly gaining acceptance.

I think we agree with Chastain (1976) that 'perhaps too much attention has been given to proper pronunciation', and we now tend to think that it is more important that the learner can communicate his ideas than that he can practice utterances with perfect pronunciation. The one thing that everyone is absolutely certain about is the necessity to use language for communicative purposes in the classroom. As early as 1968 Oller & Obrecht concluded from an experiment that communicative activity should be a central point of pattern drills from the very first stages of language learning. Savignon's (1971) widely cited dissertation confirmed that beyond doubt. Many bridle at pattern drills, but it is not very important because we agree on the basic principle of meaningful learning for the purpose of communication. And that basic principle is indicative of what may be the most significant trend: our increasing concentration on our students' learning rather than on our teaching (Oller & Richards, 1973).

In addition to the prevailing eclecticism, several new methods have gained visibility recently in the United States. In alphabetical order they are: Community Counseling Learning, Rapid Acquisition, the Silent Way, Suggestopedia, and Total Physical Response. The Monitor Model (Krashen, 1972) maybe should be mentioned here too, but at this point it is a theoretical model of language learning rather than a method for language teaching.

Community Counseling Learning or Community Language Learning (CLL) was developed by Charles A. Curran (1976) from his earlier work in affective psychology. In CLL the students sit in a circle with a tape recorder and talk about whatever interests them. The teacher whose role is seen as a counselor serves as a resource person rather than as a traditional 'teacher.' At the very beginning stages, the counselor also serves as translator for his clients: the students first utter in their native language, the teacher translates, and the students repeat their own utterancs in the L2. The tape is played back, errors analyzed and the clients copy down whatever structures they need to work on. Adherents of this method tend to be ardent in their fervor as they point out that this method teaches 'the whole person' within a supportive community which minimizes the risk-taking held necessary for language learning. Another value of this method lies in the motivational aspect in that students can talk about issues of concern to them (Stevick, 1976, 1980).

Rapid Acquisition is an approach developed by Winitz & Reeds (1973) called Rapid Acquisition of a Foreign Language by Avoidance of Speaking. The authors believe that there is a natural sequence (neurological) in language learning and stress listening comprehension until it is complete before students are allowed to speak. Length of utterance is limited, problem solving through the use of pictures are stressed, and the syllabus is limited to base structures and limited vocabulary.

The Silent Way was developed by Caleb Gattegno (1972) in 1963 but not published here until 1972. In the Silent Way, the teacher uses Cuisiniere rods, a color-coded wall chart for pronunciation, and speaks each new word only *once*; the responsibility for learning and talking is shifted to the students. Even correction is handled through gestures and mime by the teacher with no further modeling. Many teachers are enthusiastic about this method (Stevick, 1980), but I have also heard many anecdotes of student rebellion.

Suggestopedia, a method developed by Georgi Lozanov at the Institute of Suggestology in Sofia, Bulgaria (Lozanov, 1979; Bancroft, 1978) claims to reduce the stress of language learning. Listening and speaking are stressed with emphasis on vocabulary acquisition. The Suggestopedic Cycle begins with review of previously learned material in the target language, followed by introduction of new material. This is followed by a one-hour seance during which students listen to the new material against a background of baroque music. The students also do breathing exercises and yoga relaxation techniques which are said to increase concentration and tap the powers of the subconscious. There is also considerable role-play of real-life situations.

Total Physical Response, developed by James Asher (Asher, 1969; Asher & Adamski, 1977), also stresses listening comprehension as he believes that if listening and speaking are introduced simultaneously, listening comprehension is much delayed. Basically the method consists of having students listen to commands and then carry them out.

I refrain from commenting on these methods since it is not my opinion which is important but rather the teacher's. As long as teacher *and students* have confidence that they are in fact learning, and all are happy in the process, I don't think the methods make that much difference.

Conclusion

In conclusion, we can say that Newmark after all is more right than Chomsky about the significance of linguistics for the teaching of languages. But Chomsky is right too for that influence is not immediately apparent. Linguistics is like our proverbial bottom of the iceberg, mostly invisible, but massively giving shape and direction to the teaching. It took me several hours of reflection to realize that I had not heard any incorrect grammatical explanations, also an indication of linguistics at work.

Most of all linguistics becomes a worldview. It colors the approach to language, the recognition of problems and the attempts to solutions. Our TF's rejection of a formal approach to the passive, characteristic of a structural approach to linguistics, would once have been branded as mentalism, but reflects what may be the most important contribution of present day linguistics, a different attitude towards language.

Notes

1. Had I gone to a pronunciation class, I would have found lots of evidence of phonetics.
2. I understand from M. A. K. Halliday (personal communication, AILA conference, Greece 1990) that Bernstein is equally misunderstood in Britain. He is exceedingly difficult to read, but well worth the effort.
3. Speech act is a difficult concept to define and Austin (1962) and Searle (1976) have written books to do so. Hymes (1972a: 56) defines a speech act, like a joke, as the minimal term of the set speech event, a conversation, and speech situation, a party. Not that teaching speech acts is new. Kelley (1969) discusses the teaching of phrases of social life, like courting, social calls and quarreling, during the Renaissance. Shakespeare even satirized lessons from Florio. There is very little new in language teaching, except maybe the Silent Way.
4. This article was written before The Natural Approach (Krashen & Terrell, 1983). I would not want to mislead the reader that there is today general consensus on grammatical rules and explanations being beneficial. However, most scholars I know disagree with Krashen on the topic.

References

ABRAHAMS, R. and TROIKE, R. 1972, *Language and Culture Diversity in American Education.* New Jersey: Prentice-Hall.

ALBERT, M. L. and OBLER, L. K. 1978, *The Bilingual Brain: Neuropsychological and Neurolinguistic Aspects of Bilingualism.* New York: Academic Press.

ALLEN, J. P. B. and CORDER, S. P. (eds) 1975, *Papers in Applied Linguistics.* London: Oxford University Press.

ASHER, J. 1969, The total physical response approach to second language learning. *Modern Language Learning* 53, 1, 3–17.

ASHER, J. J. and ADAMSKI, C. 1977, *Learning Another Language Through Actions: The Complete Teacher's Guidebook.* Los Gatos, Calif.: Sky Oak Productions.

AUSTIN, J. L. 1962, *How To Do Things With Words.* Cambridge: Harvard University Press.

AUSUBEL, D. P. 1968, *Educational Psychology: A Cognitive View.* New York: Holt, Rinehart and Winston.

BANCROFT, W. J. 1978, The Lozanov method and its American Adaptations. *Modern Language Journal* 62, 4, 167–74.

BARATZ, J. and SHUY, R. 1969, *Teaching Black Children to Read.* Washington DC: Center for Applied Linguistics.

BEREITER, C. and ENGELMANN, S. 1966, *Teaching Disadvantaged Children in the Preschool.* Englewood Cliffs, NJ: Prentice Hall.

BERNSTEIN, B. 1971, *Class, Codes and Control* Vol. 1. London: Routledge and Kegan Paul.
—— 1972, A sociolinguistic approach to socialization; with some reference to educability. In J. GUMPERZ and D. HYMES (eds) *Directions in Sociolinguistics.* New York: Holt, Rinehart and Winston.
—— 1973, *Class, Codes and Control* Vol. 2. London: Routledge and Kegan Paul.
BORKIN, A. and REINHART, S. 1978, Excuse me and I'm sorry. *TESOL Quarterly* 12, 57–70.
BROWN, D. 1974, Editorial. *Language Learning* 24, 2, v–vi.
BROWN, R. A. 1973, *A First Language: The Early Stages.* Cambridge, Mass.: University Press.
BRUMFIT, C. 1981, Notional syllabuses revisited: a response. *Applied Linguistics* 2, 190–2.
BRUMFIT, C. and JOHNSON, K. (eds) 1979, *The Communicative Approach to Language Teaching.* Oxford: Oxford University Press.
BURGER, H. 1971, *Ethno-Pedagogy: Cross-Cultural Teaching Techniques.* Albuquerque, NM: Southwestern Cooperative Educational Laboratory.
CANALE, M. and SWAIN, M. 1979, *Communicative Approaches to Second Language Teaching and Testing.* Ontario: Ministry of Education.
CANDLIN, C. (ed.) 1975, *The Communicative Teaching of English.* London: Longman.
CARRELL, P. and KONNEKER, B. 1981, Politeness: comparing native and nonnative judgments. *Language Learning* 31, 17–30.
CARROLL, J. B. 1971, Current issues in psycholinguistics and second language teaching. *TESOL Quarterly* 5, 2, 101–17.
—— 1974, Learning theory for the classroom teacher. In G. A. JARVIS (ed.) *The Challenge of Communication.* Skokie, Ill.: National Textbook Company.
CAZDEN, C. B., JOHN, V. P. and HYMES, D. (eds) 1972, *Functions of Language in the Classroom.* New York: Teachers College Press.
CHASTAIN, K. 1976, *Developing Second-Language Skills: Theory to Practice* 2nd edn. Chicago: Rand, McNally.
CHOMSKY, N. 1966, Linguistic theory. *Language Teaching: Broader Contexts.* Northeast Conference on the Teaching of Foreign Languages.
CLARK, H. E. and CLARK, E. V. 1977, *Psychology and Language.* New York: Harcourt Brace Jovanovich.
CORDER, S. P. 1973, *Introducing Applied Linguistics.* Baltimore: Penguin.
—— 1975, Applied linguistics and language teaching. In J. P. B. ALLEN and S. P. CORDER (eds) *Papers in Applied Linguistics.* London: Oxford University Press.
CURRAN, C. A. 1976, *Counseling-Learning in Second Languages.* Apple River, Ill.: Apple River Press.
DATO, D. (ed.) 1975, *Developmental Psycholinguistics: Theory and Applications.* Georgetown University Round Table on Languages and Linguistics. Washington, DC: Georgetown University Press.
DILLARD, J. L. 1972, *Black English: Its History and Usage in the United States.* New York: Vintage Books.
ERVIN-TRIPP, S. 1976, Is Sybil there? The structure of some American English directives. *Language in Society* 5, 25–66.
FEIGENBAUM, J. 1970, The use of nonstandard English in teaching standard: contrast and comparison. In R. W. FASOLD and R. W. SHUY (eds) *Teaching Standard English in the Inner City.* Washington, DC: Center for Applied Linguistics.

FRIES, C. C. 1945, *Teaching and Learning English as a Foreign Language*. Ann Arbor: University of Michigan Press.

FUREY, P. 1972, Grammar explanations in foreign language teaching. Unpublished MA thesis, University of Pittsburgh.

GATTEGNO, C. 1972, *Teaching Foreign Languages in Schools the Silent Way* 2nd edn. New York: Educational Solutions.

GLEASON, H. A. Jr, 1955, *An Introduction to Descriptive Linguistics*. New York: Holt, Rinehart and Winston.

GRIMSHAW, D. 1973, Rules, social interaction and language behavior. *TESOL Quarterly* 7, 2, 109.

HYMES, D. 1967, The anthropology of communication. In F. DANCE (ed.) *Human Communication Theory*. New York: Holt, Rinehart and Winston.

—— 1972a, Models of the interaction of language and social life. In J. GUMPERZ and D. HYMES (eds) *Directions in Sociolinguistics*. New York: Holt, Rinehart and Winston.

—— 1972b, Introduction. In C. CAZDEN, V. JOHN and D. HYMES (eds) *The Function of Language in the Classroom* (p. xi–lviii). New York: Teachers College Press.

—— 1972c, On communicative competence. In J. B. PRIDE and J. HOLMES (eds) *Sociolinguistics* (pp. 269–93). Harmondsworth, England: Penguin Books.

—— 1974, *Foundations in Sociolinguistics*. Philadelphia: University of Pennsylvania Press.

JENSEN, A. 1969, How much can we boost IQ and scholastic achievement? *Harvard Educational Review* 39, 1.

JOHNSON, K. and MORROW, K. 1978, *Communicate*. Reading: University of Reading.

—— 1979, *Approaches*. Cambridge: Cambridge University Press.

KELLEY, L. G. 1969, *25 Centuries of Language Teaching*. Rowley, Mass.: Newbury House.

KOCHMAN, T. (ed.) 1972, *Rappin' and Stylin' Out: Communication in Urban Black America*. Chicago: University of Illinois Press.

KRASHEN, S. D. 1972, The Monitor Model for adult second language performance. In M. BURT, H. DULAY and M. FINOCCHIARO (eds) *Viewpoints on English Language as a Second Language* (pp. 152–61). New York: Regents.

KRASHEN, S. D. and TERRELL, T. D. 1983, *The Natural Approach*. Hayward, CA: Alemany Press.

LABOV, W. 1969, *The Study of Non-Standard English*. Washington DC: ERIC, Center for Applied Linguistics.

LACKSTROM, J., SELINKER, L. and TRIMBLE, L. 1970, Grammar and technical English. *English as a Second Language: Current Issues*. Chilton Press.

LADO, R. 1957, *Linguistics Across Cultures: Applied Linguistics for Teachers*. Ann Arbor: University of Michigan Press.

LAKOFF, R. 1969, Transformational grammar and language teaching. *Language Learning* 19, 1 and 2, 117–40.

—— 1974, Linguistic theory and the real world. Paper presented at the TESOL Convention 1974, Denver, Colorado.

LARSEN-FREEMAN, D. 1981, The 'what' of second language acquisition. In M. HINES and W. RUTHERFORD (eds) *On TESOL '81*. Washington, DC: TESOL.

LENNEBERG, E. H. and LENNEBERG, E. (eds) 1975, *Foundations of Language Development*. New York: Academic Press.

LEVINSON, S. 1980, Speech act theory: the state of the art. *Language Teaching and Linguistic Abstracts* 13, 5–24.

LOZANOV, G. 1979, *Suggestology and Outlines of Suggestopedy*. New York: Gordon and Breach.

MITCHELL-KERNAN, C. 1971, *Language Behavior in a Black Urban Community*. Monographs of the Language-Behavior Research Laboratory No. 2, University of California at Berkeley.

MOULTON, W. G. 1961, Linguistics and language teaching in the United States, 1940–1960. In C. MOHEMANN, *et al.* (eds) *Trends in European and American Linguistics*. Utrecht: Spectrum.

—— 1970, *A Linguistic Guide to Language Learning* 2nd edn. New York: Modern Language Association.

MUNBY, J. 1978, *Communicative Syllabus Design*. Cambridge: Cambridge University Press.

NEWMARK, L. 1970, Grammatical theory and the teaching of English as a foreign language. In M. LESTER (ed.) *Readings in Applied Transformational Grammar*. New York: Holt, Rinehart and Winston.

NIDA, E. A. 1949, *Morphology: The Descriptive Analysis of Words*. Ann Arbor, Mich.: University of Michigan Press.

—— 1954, *Customs and Cultures*. New York: Harper.

NILSEN, D. L. F. 1971, The use of case grammar in teaching English as a foreign language. *TESOL Quarterly* 5, 4, 293–300.

NORRIS, W. 1972, *TESOL at the Beginning of the 70's: Trends, Topics, and Research Needs*. Pittsburgh, PA: University Center for International Studies.

OLLER, J. and OBRECHT, D. H. 1968, Pattern drill and communicative activity: a psycholinguistic experiment. *IRAL* 6, 2, 165–72.

OLLER, J. W. Jr and RICHARDS, J. C. (eds) 1973, *Focus on the Learner: Pragmatic Perspectives for the Language Teachers*. Rowley, Mass.: Newbury House.

PAULSTON, C. B. 1970, Teaching footnotes and bibliographical entries to foreign students: a tagmemic approach. *English Language Teaching* 34–3.

—— 1981, Notional syllabuses revisited: some comments. *Applied Linguistics* 2, 1, 93–5.

PIKE, K. 1947, *Phonemics: A Technique for Reducing Languages to Writing*. Ann Arbor: University of Michigan Press.

QUIRK, R. and GREENBAUM, S. 1973, *A Concise Grammar of Contemporary English*. New York: Harcourt, Brace, Jovanovich.

QUIRK, R., GREENBAUM, S., LEECH, G. and SVARTVIK, J. 1972, *A Grammar of Contemporary English*. New York: Seminar Press.

RICHARDS, J. C. 1974, *Error Analysis: Perspectives on Second Language Acquisition*. London: Longman.

—— (ed.) 1976, *Teaching English for Science and Technology*. Singapore: RELC.

RIEBER, R. W. 1976, *The Neuropsychology of Language*. New York: Plenum Press.

RINTELL, E. 1979, Getting your speech act together: The pragmatic ability of second language learners. *Working Papers on Bilingualism* 17, 97–106.

ROULET, E. 1975, *Linguistic Theory, Linguistic Description, and Language Teaching*. London: Longman.

ROULET, E. and HOLEC, H. 1976, *L'Enseignement de la competence de communication en langues secondes*. Neuchatel: Universite de Neuchatel.

RUTHERFORD, W. 1968, *Modern English*. New York: Harcourt, Brace and World.

SAVIGNON, S. 1971, Study of the effect of training in communicative skills as part of a beginning college French course on student attitude and achievement in linguistic and communicative competence. Ph.D. dissertation, University of Illinois at Urbana-Champaign.

SAVILLE-TROIKE, M. 1976, *Foundations for Teaching English as a Second Language: Theory and Method for Multicultural Education*. Englewood Cliffs, NJ: Prentice-Hall.

SCARCELLA, R. 1979, On speaking politely in a second language. In C. YORIO, K. PERKINS and J. SCHACTER (eds) *On TESOL '79*. Washington, DC: TESOL.

SCHACHTER, J. 1974, An error in error analysis. *Language Learning* 24, 2, 205–14, 213.

SEARLE, J. 1976, A classification of illocutionary acts. *Language in Society* 5, 1–25.

SELINKER, L., TRIMBLE L. and VROMAN, R. 1972, *Working Papers in Scientific and Technical English*. University of Washington: Office of Engineering Research.

SHUY, R. and FASOLD, R. 1970, *Teaching Standard English in the Inner City*. Washington, DC: Center for Applied Linguistics.

SLOBIN, D. I. 1971, *Psycholinguistics*. Glenview, Ill.: Scott, Foresman & Co.

SPOLSKY, B. 1969, Linguistics and language pedagogy — applications or implications? In Georgetown University Round Table 22, 143–55.

—— (ed.) 1972, The Education of Minority Children. Rowley, Mass.: Newbury House.

—— 1978, *Educational Linguistics*. Rowley, Mass.: Newbury House.

STEVICK, E. 1976, *Memory, Meaning and Method: Some Psychological Perspectives on Language Learning*. Rowley, Mass.: Newbury House.

—— 1980, *Teaching Languages: A Way and Ways*. Rowley, Mass.: Newbury House.

TAYLOR, I. 1976, *Introduction to Psycholinguistics*. New York: Holt, Rinehart and Winston.

TRUEBA, H. and BARNETT-MIGRAHI, C. (eds) 1979, *Bilingual Multicultural Education and the Professional*. Rowley, Mass.: Newbury House.

VAN EK, J. A. 1978, *The Threshold Level of Modern Language Teaching in Schools*. Longmans.

WALTERS, J. 1979, Strategies for requesting in Spanish and English. *Language Learning* 29, 277–93.

WARDHAUGH, R. 1969, Teaching English to speakers of other languages: the State of the Art. Washington, DC: ERIC Clearinghouse for Linguistics, Center for Applied Linguistics, ED 030119.

WARRINER, J. E., WHITTEN, M. E. and GRIFFITH, F. 1975, *English Grammar and Composition*. New York: Harcourt, Brace, Jovanovich.

WIDDOWSON, H. 1978, *Teaching Language as Communication*. London: Oxford University Press.

WILKINS, D. A. 1976, *Notional Syllabuses*. Oxford: Oxford University Press.

WINITZ, H. and REEDS, J. A. 1973, Rapid acquisition of a foreign language by avoidance of speaking. *IRAL* 11, 4, 295–317.

WOLFRAM, W. 1969, *A Sociolinguistic Description of Detroit Negro Speech*. Washington, DC: Center for Applied Linguistics.

WOLFRAM, W. and CLARKE, N. 1971, *Black–White Speech Relationships*. Washington, DC: Center for Applied Linguistics.

WOLFSON, N. 1981, Compliments in cross-cultural perspective. *TESOL Quarterly* 15, 2, 117–24.

10 Communicative Competence and Language Teaching: Second Thoughts

Introduction and Background

It is frequently commented that it takes some 20 years for new academic concepts and insights to become commonplace in the teaching of our public schools. That is also the case with the notion of communicative competence and language teaching. Twenty years ago Gumperz & Hymes (1964) edited a special issue of the *American Anthropologist* with the title of 'The ethnography of communication'. This publication was the basis of their later *Directions in Sociolinguistics: The Ethnography of Communication* (1972) of which 'the theoretical goal . . . is best illustrated by the notion of communicative competence: what a speaker needs to know to communicate effectively in culturally significant settings' (Gumperz & Hymes, 1972: vii). Ten years ago I wrote an article 'Linguistic and communicative competence' (Paulston, 1974 — see Chapter 5, this volume) which I believe was the first attempt to work out the implications for language teaching from Dell Hymes' (1972) notion of communicative competence. The time has come to take stock.

The concern for communicative language teaching surfaced on both sides of the Atlantic as early as the late 1960s (Oller & Obrecht, 1968; Jakobovits, 1969; Rutherford, 1968; Wardhaugh, 1969; etc.). Partially it was a reaction against the mechanical nature and boring activity of drills in the audio-lingual method, but communicative competence was also a counter-concept to Chomsky's (1957) notion of competence in theoretical linguistics. In my own work, I joined an insistence on using language at least some of the time for communicative purposes (Paulston, 1970; see also Chapter 2, this volume), with, later, a rationale firmly based on Hymes' communicative competence (Paulston, 1974).

What do we mean by communicative competence in language teaching? People mean two different things with it, and it is often confusing because it is not clear which definition they had in mind. Rivers (1973) and those who work with foreign language teaching in the United States tend to define communicative competence as simply linguistic interaction in the target language: 'the ability to function in a truly communicative setting; that is, in a spontaneous transaction involving one or more other persons' (Savignon, 1978: 12). People who work in ESL, on the other hand, tend to use communicative competence in Hymes' sense to include not only the linguistic forms of the language but also its social rules, the knowledge of when, how, and to whom it is appropriate to use these forms. In the latter view, the objectives of language teaching are held to include the socio-cultural rules for language use, not as an added cultural component, but as an integral part of the language taught. To wit, there are rules in American English not only for forming grammatically correct wh-questions but also for the topic of questions which are admissable and socially appropriate. A Japanese banker some years ago when I was promoted to associate professor asked me how old I was to be so promoted. I simply did not answer his question because I thought it was both inappropriate and inadmissable. I told him instead that age had nothing to do with it which he, in his turn, found a very peculiar remark.

Finally, in addition to these two common definitions of communicative competence in language teaching, for purposes of research Canale & Swain (1979, 1980) in their review of the literature on communicative competence suggest three subcomponents: grammatical, discourse, and sociolinguistic competence, which together make up communicative competence. Grammatical competence is just that, a knowledge of lexical items and the rules of morphology, syntax, sentence-grammar semantics, and phonology (Canale & Swain, 1979: 54). Discourse competence is 'defined as the ability to produce and recognize coherent and cohesive text' (Canale & Swain, 1983: 5) while sociolinguistic competence is 'defined as the ability to produce and recognize socially appropriate language within a given socio-cultural context (p. 9), i.e. Hymes' social rules of language use. This tripartite definition makes possible a more precise testing in the proficiency of communicative competence.

The title of this conference, 'Communicative Language Teaching' (CLT) wisely begs the question and allows whatever definition you choose to work with. That choice is important and will to a considerable degree decide goals and objectives as well as syllabi and curriculum of language teaching. In the remainder of this paper I will use communicative competence as I have always done to refer to the anthropological sense of socio-cultural rules for language use and use CLT primarily to refer to spontaneous oral interaction in general.

Methods and Language Teaching

Now, there is very little new in language teaching as a quick perusal of Kelly's (1969) *25 Centuries of Language Teaching* will attest to. St Augustine introduced the use of dialogues, there were pattern drills in the Middle Ages, the scholastics taught patterns of politeness and rudeness in a sort of notional/functional approach (only of course, they didn't call it that), grammar-translation goes back to the Greeks and before. Even the Hittites 2000 BC did grammar translation. There is a limit on what a teacher can do to a class; there are just so many activities students can undertake in a classroom, and with the exception of new technological advances, there is very little new at the technique level. (Except, maybe, the Silent Way.)

What does change is the combination and constellation of techniques into methods as well as all the theories that attempt to account for them. The fact of the matter is that we really don't know how to account for language acquisition, and so we have a lot of theories which come and go. We also have some remarkable methods at present and you can make the case that communicative language teaching is a method. How do we take stock?[1]

Jack Richards (1983) in his plenary TESOL address 'The secret life of methods' points out that facts have very little to do with the evaluation of methods:

> This rarely followed option involves empirical demonstration of the validity of a method's claims, for example, through documented research which demonstrates precisely what learners achieve as a result of instruction. This route is difficult to carry out, and since its findings may not necessarily be the ones we hoped for, there is little of it in the literature. Consequently, there is not a single serious piece of research published to demonstrate precisely what learners learn from a Notional syllabus, from Communicative Language Teaching, Silent Way, or most of the other methods which countless journal articles advocate with such enthusiasm. (Richards, 1983: 11)

Richards is right, with one exception, that we really have no data as to teaching efficacy to support all the enthusiastic claims of this spate of new sometimes called humanistic methods. The exception is communicative language teaching. As early as 1968, Oller & Obrecht (1968) concluded from an experimental study that communicative activity should be a central point of pattern drills from the very first stages of language learning. Savignon's widely cited dissertation in 1971 confirmed beyond doubt that language learning which used language for purposes of communication, for getting messages across, was a more efficient process of learning than the audio-lingual type pattern drills. But Richards is right that we don't know how communicative language teaching compares with any of the other recent methods on the basis of facts. It seems inconceivable to me that some of these new methods would be a more efficient way of teaching language but there are no data to prove it one way or the other.

So stock taking in a scientific fashion based on hard data from experimental comparisons becomes impossible. How then can I make a judgment? Basically, I can know in two ways acceptable to academics: through practical experience and empirical evidence or through theoretical speculations or knowledge of others' theory and model building, the linking of constructs into propositions and interrelated hypotheses. Teachers have in time honored fashion through trial and error sorted out in their classroom what will and will not work, even though they do not necessarily know why and how it works. It is an empiricism, born of the necessity of the teaching situation, which is basically divorced from theory. As such, it has very little prestige in academia. Prestige lies with theoretical speculations of the kind which allows me to reason, for example, that the importance of the role which we assign these days to input in the language acquisition process will argue against a method which limits the teacher's utterance of a new word to one occurrence as it does in the Silent Way. Preferably you want your theory to explain your empirical data, but if I had to choose one or the other — and I am now only talking about language teaching and learning of which we know so very little — I would prefer the judgment of common sense classroom teachers to that of theoretical speculations. Ignoring teacher judgments can be an expensive proposition.

Current theories of language acquisition very much support communicative activities in the classroom but there are no learning theories which can be stretched to motivate communicative competence in Hymes' sense. The theories for the latter come from anthropology and support *what* should be taught, not *how*. Since we can draw on neither learning theories nor empirical evidence, we are reduced to practical experience and common sense in making our claims and judgment about communicative competence in language teaching, no more, no less.

I want to conclude this section of my paper with two comments on methods in general. One is that methods probably are not very important in accounting for language learning results. Given the social setting and the super/subordinate relationship between ethnic groups which contribute to one learning the other's language, given what it takes to provide opportunity and motivation, it is very unlikely that methods will play any greater importance. That is probably another reason[2] why it is so difficult to get conclusive evidence in experimental design research comparing various methods. As Lennart Levin (1969) concluded, tongue in cheek, after a major Swedish study 'All methods are best'.

The other comment is to explain the at times puzzling popularity of many of the new methods. You can with Kuhn (1971) talk of paradigm shift in the sciences and sketch the anatomy of the Chomskyan revolution which did have a great influence in toppling the audio-lingual school of thought, or you can simply talk of fashions in language teaching which like our skirt lengths go up and down. Skirt lengths have nothing to do with common sense and Suggestopedia is in vogue.[3] Nor does it have anything to do with common sense.

Second Thoughts

Where does all this leave us with language teaching and communicative competence? I do indeed have second thoughts. I regret to say that I think we have gone too far, and that the swing of the pendulum of high fashion has carried us off the Middle Road of good judgment and common sense. I have three reasons for this concern.

The first two reasons both have to do with the material to be taught, with the specific teaching points. I am not here really concerned with whether the syllabus should be organized according to a structural/linguistic content or according to functions and speech acts, although that is a very important matter that has never been satisfactorily worked out.[4] In any case it is a topic for last year's '83 conference.

The problem lies with the basic description of speech acts and the rules for their usage. The ten years since I wrote 'Linguistic and communicative competence' (Paulston, 1974) I have partly spent directing and supervising MA theses on speech acts and the teaching of English. If native speakers after two years of intense study of theoretical and applied linguistics and sociolinguistics not only do not themselves know these rules but also find immense difficulties in ascertaining and describing them maybe we should be a little more careful than I was ten years ago in globally prescribing a communicative competence approach in language teaching.

The difficulty of description does not basically lie at the theoretical level. Hymes' framework is holding up very well and further work, like Brown & Levinson (1978) add useful support.

The difficulty lies partially in the difficulty of observation and collection of data and in the selection of variables which influence language manifestations. Labov's paradox of how you observe unobserved behavior is of concern here. At present a student of mine is studying rejoinders to *thank you*. Degree of formality is likely to be a variable and she can in all likelihood collect data in situations where setting will trigger register, like court and church. But social class is also likely to be a variable and she simply will not be able to unobtrusively observe in-group upper-class behavior in Pittsburgh. This is not the place to discuss how you deal with such problems but they are very real and very much there.

Another difficulty lies with the variability of the communicative competence rules. The range of rejoinders to *thank you* suprises me, not just the American *you are welcome* (dialectal variation) but *ah ha* and *OK* (generational variation?), the latter which I would until recently have denied as native usage. In order to teach communicative competence, core norms, which are hard to find, must be captured and given a significant generalization. What happens very often is that teachers disagree with the rules in the text, refuse to teach them and criticize the text, a situation which is very confusing to the students. Teaching communicative competence is not as simple as we once thought.

The second reason for my concern about teaching English for communicative competence in a city like Singapore is the problem of whose rules. In Pittsburgh that is easy. Our students in the English Language Institute do need to learn general American rules for using language in interaction and negotiating meaning in socially appropriate ways. Our Latin American students need not only to know the phrase for *thank you* but also that they shouldn't repeat it ten times because then they sound insincere in English, and our Japanese students will have to learn to turn down requests from superiors. A while back I wanted to change an appointment with a doctoral student who happened to be Japanese, asked if she could come right after class instead of 2 p.m. as we had planned, she said yes and came. Months later in a report to our sociolinguistic class, she treated this episode as data, went on to relate that she had had a luncheon date with a friend waiting on a street corner, but Japanese rules made it impossible for her to say no to me. (Luckily the friend was Japanese too and understood why she was stood up.) I, of course, would never even think it noticeable if she had told me that she had another appointment. The point of this anecdote is that living in a specific culture, your life can become unnecessarily complicated without attention to the communicative competence rules of language.

When I lived in Lima and made an appointment with a Peruvian, I always said 'Your rules or mine?' so I would know whether to be on time or late. They always understood what I meant and themselves routinely used the expressions *hora latina, hora gringa* 'latin time, foreign time' for clarification. The point here is that one set of rules was not perceived as better than another, it was simply a practical matter of clearing noise in the channel, of functioning with the same rules.

But for a Swede being on time[5] is not just a practical concern but one of moral implications. To be late is to show moral weakness, and so it is with many of the communicative competence rules that they don't only signal social meaning but that they also reflect the values and belief system of the culture in which they are operative. My Japanese student's inability to say no to me was not just a question of quaint etiquette but is solidly founded on Japanese worldview and value system.

Now maybe you are beginning to see my concern. To insist in Singapore that speakers behave with English in a way that is culturally appropriate in the United States and which reflects American values is just plain silly. In the first place, there are perfectly legitimate — and different — British and Australian ways of using English that cannot just be ignored. In the second place, English is an official language in Singapore, and as Braj Kachru has argued for years for Indian English, Singaporean English has a right to its own life, to its own local communicative competence. To argue anything else sounds to me very much like cultural imperialism, and I hope nobody took seriously the article of mine which RELC published a few years ago (Paulston, 1979). I recant. I think now that English belongs every bit as much to those who use it as a lingua franca, as a language of wider communication (LWC), as it does to the English-speaking peoples. The use of English in Singapore is an economic and political statement of citizens of the free world, not a cultural orientation toward Britain or the United States.

In the third place, it is silly because it is unrealistic. Asian culture is enormously tenacious, and even if every USIS and British Council member descended on Singapore to preach the virtues of a communicative competence approach in ESL, I doubt that it would make any difference. People in Singapore — and India and Nigeria and Hong Kong — will go on speaking English with the communicative competence rules of their native tongue,[6] and I think we should accept that fact as a positive state of affairs.

Finally, my third reason for concern applies to all communicative language teaching, not just to matters of communicative competence. It concerns teacher competencies. As Richards & Rodgers (1982) discuss in an excellent article on methods of language teaching, different methods require different roles of teachers and students. In the audio-lingual method, the teacher controlled all activities, and closely tied to his textbook, he conducted the orchestra of his class. Breen & Candlin discuss the role of the teacher in a communicative approach which is to facilitate communication and act as independent participant:

> These roles imply a set of secondary roles for the teacher; first, as an organizer of resources and as a resource himself, second as a guide within the classroom procedures and activities . . . A third role for the teacher is that of researcher and learner, with much to contribute in terms of appropriate knowledge and abilities, actual and observed experience of the nature of learning, and organizational capacities. (Breen & Candlin, 1980: 99)

In short, what communicative language teaching requires (much as the Direct Method did before it) in order to be effective is teachers with near-native competence in English. It is all very well to have communicative language teaching be the rage in Britain and the United States where the teachers are native speakers of English but quite another matter to export it to parts of the world which routinely use non-native speakers of English. I don't know how many of you have ever taught a language you knew imperfectly but I remember vividly teaching French in Pine Island, Minnesota. The textbook was my lifeline and I certainly did not encourage student questions about vocabulary items as the likelihood that I wouldn't know the answer was high. It is just plain scary for teachers to be in front of a class and not know what they are teaching. Add to the requirement of teacher fluency in the target language, cultural values of saving face and the position of teachers in the social hierarchy (i.e. teachers command high respect and it is difficult for them to admit to ignorance), and it seems to me that a great deal of caution is needed in adopting a communicative approach in ESL in Southeast Asia. A demoralized teacher corps is not conducive to effective language teaching.

Effective Classroom Techniques

I suggested earlier that methods are not very important, so maybe a method of communicative language teaching does not make much difference. But I do think that techniques and procedures in language teaching *are* important, that classroom activities and how they are conducted *will* influence learning. I say that methods are not important because there is no one-to-one relationship between method and techniques. For instance, dialogues in language teaching have been around since St Augustine's days and have been used in different methods for different purposes.

What I would like to do at this point is to examine some features of effective classroom activities from an unusual ethnographic descriptive study of bilingual education. I want to do this in order to see how many of these features we find in communicative language learning. The Significant Bilingual Instructional Features (SBIF) study is a three year study, funded by the (US) National Institute of Education, and just completed. The intent of the study is 'to provide important information that will increase understanding of bilingual instruction, and subsequently increase opportunities for students with limited or no proficiency in English to participate fully and successfully in the educational process' (Tikunoff, 1983: v). It will eventually become available through ERIC, but in the meantime I would like to share some of the findings and their implications for ESL and communicative language teaching as I think it is an important study.

In contrast to all the experimental-design, psychometric studies of language teaching methods, this study identified successful teachers[7] and then observed their 58 classrooms for significant instructional features.[8] Five features were found to be significant and they all have to do with teaching behaviors rather than curriculum or materials. (See Appendix.) 'Regardless of variation in programs, curriculum and materials, school district policies, philosophies of instruction, and ethnolinguistic groups, the teachers in the sample exhibited all five features frequently and consistently' (Tikunoff, 1983: 6). It may be fashionable to minimize the teacher's role in the classroom, but I think it is a serious mistake. The SBIF study documents beyond any reasonable doubt the importance of teacher behavior, not of methods and materials but of classroom procedures and activities.

In discussing the SBIF findings, I will extrapolate those features which relate to language learning. The SBIF study was concerned with successful learning in general.

In reading through the 15 documents of the study, my strongest impression was that *the* most important teaching characteristic is efficient classroom management. I think most of us would agree that one of the teacher's major roles is to structure the school environment so that the students can learn, which is what good classroom management does. Good teaching allows for both learning and acquisition.[9] Learning would include activities which focused on form, such as reading aloud in English with the focus on sound-symbol relationship, working with vocabulary cards, copying sentences where the right word had to be filled in (these activities are taken from the SBIF study), while acquisition presumably takes place during activities where the focus is on the content or function of language, such as free compositions, role-plays, and interaction activities. The acquisition process is in fact the major theoretical rationale for a communicative approach, and the evidence is quite clear that without a stage of language use for communication, language teaching is not very efficient (Savignon, 1971; Swain, 1983). It is the teacher's job to arrange for both types of activities in the classroom.

Good teachers make very clear what tasks and exercises they set and what the students must do to accomplish these tasks. They were careful to explain, outline, summarize and review. The teachers also gave a lot of attention to vocabulary work. In second language acquisition, learners probably focus on vocabulary and then work out the semantic relationship between lexical items (and the grammar) from their pragmatic knowledge of the real world. In any case, it is clear from the SBIF study that good teachers spend a lot of energy, their own and students', on vocabulary development. The easiest way for a student to understand the meaning of a new word in the L2 is through translation to his mother tongue, and the SBIF teachers routinely used the children's mother tongue if they got lost or confused. Half the time this was to individual students and it was a reiteration or translation of what they had not understood in English the first time. Clearly the ESL teacher needs to exercise judgment here. We certainly don't want long linguistic lectures in the L1 but on the other hand we don't want long linguistic lectures in English either. If a gloss or two or a brief sentence in the L1 would save time and clarify, then I think it is justified. If some students get lost during a role-play, then a quick *sotto voce* L1 explanation might be helpful. What is perfectly clear is that the students must understand what is going on.

They must also work. The SBIF study measured Academic Learning Time (ALT), the time a student is productively engaged in completing assigned tasks at a relatively high rate of accuracy. These students were productively engaged for as much as 82% of the time, which is amazingly high in that it only allows the teacher 18% of the time for instruction, explanations, directions, etc. The most common fault of language teachers is teacher talk. The most appealing aspect of communicative language teaching is that the very method dictates against teacher talk. (And I have also had teachers who say that they don't like to do role-plays with their class because it leaves them out, they are not center of the stage any more.) But whatever the method, it is the students who need to process language, not the teacher. Swain (1983) argues convincingly in a recent paper that comprehensible output is as necessary a source for grammatical acquisition as is comprehensible input. Good language teachers keep their students working hard on tasks they understand and which are intrinsically interesting to them.

Now the truth of the matter is that most normal people don't find language learning tasks very interesting. One of the advantages of communicative language teaching is that many of the classroom activities are a lot more interesting than grammar drills and fill-in-the-slot exercises so that whether or not the students learn any more, motivation and attention remain higher. But any activity done too long or too often will stale and that is every bit as true of role-plays as of dialogues. The answer lies with a multiple of activities and a change of pace. Keeping students working hard and willingly on task is very much the art of teaching but it also takes careful planning and structure.

Good teachers also make sure that students know what constitutes successful performance so that they know when they are achieving success or they are given access to information about how to achieve success. ALT specifies a high degree of accuracy and the SBIF findings are that 'students who are responding incorrectly to a task need immediate feedback concerning those responses' (Tikunoff, 1983: 12). This is true for reading and mathematics, but linguists see errors as an inevitable by-product of second language acquisition. This leaves the question of what teachers are supposed to do with errors in the classroom.

One argument is immediate feedback and correction, as the study findings suggest. Another argument claims that students will learn only if they feel secure affectively and that therefore error correction is ineffectual and tension creating and that students should be left alone to experiment creatively with the second language. There are no experimental data on the role of error correction in L2 acquisition in bilingual education so once again the ESL teacher has to make decisions based on judgment rather than fact.

The guidelines we use for correction in the English language Institute are the following: if the error is directly part of the teaching point, whether formal like the pronunciation of plurals or functional like the use of present habitual or present progressive, it is helpful in clarifying input to provide immediate feedback and correction. I don't believe that error correction needs to be tension creating; errors and correction are part of school life. But when errors occur incidentally to what is being taught, and they don't interfere with communication or classroom procedures, then I think they are not very important and can be safely ignored. As usual, tact and common sense will tell us more about error correction than research will at the present.

Conclusion

In conclusion, the findings from the SBIF study make the following reflections seem feasible. Good teachers do make a difference. Methods and materials are not as important as principles of meaningful and interesting activities, on-task focus, clear activity objectives and comprehensible feedback.[10] To the degree that teachers can incorporate these principles in their classroom activities, their students should learn English, but it seems that communicative language teaching by its nature already does or easily can incorporate all of these features. A communicative competence approach to language teaching in Singapore may not be very sensible, but hopefully an approach to language teaching which incorporates genuine communication in the classroom will prove to be more than a fad.

Appendix

Five instructional features

The five instructional features identified as significant for the instruction of LEP students are described as follows.

1. Successful teachers of LEP students exhibit a *congruence of instructional intent, organization and delivery of instruction, and student consequences.* They specify task outcomes and what students must do to accomplish tasks competently. In addition, they communicate (a) high expectations for LEP students in terms of learning, and (b) a sense of efficacy in terms of their own ability to teach.
2. Successful teachers of LEP students, like effective teachers generally, exhibit *use of active teaching behaviors* which have been found to be related to increased student performance on academic tests of achievement in reading and mathematics. These active teaching behaviors include (a) communicating clearly when giving directions, specifying tasks, and presenting new information — communication may involve such strategies as explaining, outlining, or demonstrating; (b) obtaining and maintaining students' engagement in instructional tasks by pacing instruction appropriately, promoting involvement, and communicating their expectations for students' success in completing instructional tasks; (c) monitoring students' progress, and (d) providing immediate feedback whenever required regarding the students' success.
3. Successful teachers of LEP students mediate instruction for LEP students by the *use of the students' native language (L1) and English (L2) for instruction,* alternating between the two languages whenever necessary to ensure clarity of instruction for LEP students.
4. Successful teachers of LEP students mediate instruction for LEP students by the *integration of English language development with basic skills instruction,* focusing on LEP students acquiring English terms for concepts and lesson content even when L1 is used for a portion of the instruction.

5. Successful teachers of LEP students mediate instruction in a third way by the *use of information from the LEP students' home culture*. They (a) utilize cultural referents during instruction; (b) organize instruction to build upon participant structures from the LEP students' home culture, and (c) observe the values and norms of the LEP students' home culture even as the norms of the majority culture are being taught.

(Tikunoff, 1983: 6–7)

Notes

1. I don't want to get side-tracked into discussing methods but it is clear that different methods do different things: the notional/functional syllabus specifies the teaching points but with no word about *how* to teach them; community counseling learning modifies the role relationship between teacher and student into counselor and client but leaves the syllabus unspecified; grammar/translation specified both teaching points and activities but never dealt with how the teacher would get that mass of linguistic information (often faulty) across to the students. The audio-lingual method was rare in its attention to all aspects of language teaching: syllabus, teacher behavior, student behavior, classroom activities, linguistic description, and indeed what went on in the heads of the students.

   Communicative language teaching as a method specifies the nature of the classroom interaction/activities and sometimes the teaching points (primarily in the units of speech acts) (e.g. Munby, 1978).

   Francis Johnson points out that since methods in fact attempt different things, it is frequently misleading to compare methods. His point is that a method which has as its main objective helping children learn language acquisition strategies should not be compared with a method whose objective is the memorization of vocabulary and grammar rules, using the same criteria of evaluation (personal communication, April, 1984). I quite agree.
2. The first being that methods do different things and are therefore difficult to compare on the same results.
3. The reasons for that vogue is another matter. The need for new dissertation topics and tenure is one probable reason. I suspect teachers just get plain bored doing the same thing year in and year out, i.e. classroom experimentation as a way of self renewal. It is certainly one way to read Stevick (1980).
4. My own preference for adult learners is for a syllabus organized according to a structional/linguistic content, where the criteria for selection and sequencing of patterns derive from functions firmly grounded in situations which are based on a needs assessment where possible.
5. More than five minutes past the appointed time is beginning to be late. Since such split second timing is difficult in the modern world, Swedes often arrive early and walk around the block so they can enter at the exact time.

   1991 postscript: I suspect the Swedes may be becoming internationalized in regards to extreme punctuality. For those with much international experience, it may have taken on aspects of chic to be 10, 15 minutes late, but then this is speculation. I do know that I have recently observed such behavior.
6. Or some combination of rules of local language.

7. The teachers were nominated as successful by principals, teachers and parents.
8. 'To be significant, an instructional feature had to meet four criteria. First, it has to be relevant in the research literature in terms of positive instructional consequences for LEP students. Second, it had to have occurred frequently and to a high degree in the classes. Third, it must have been identified by teachers in the sample during their analysis of their own instruction as being significant . . . Fourth, during analysis, features or clusters of features had to be associated with desirable consequences for LEP students.' (Tikunoff, 1983: 6).
9. Learning is the result of teaching while acquisition results from the student's processing of meaningful language input (Krashen, 1981). Many believe that without the opportunity for acquisition, a second language is not likely to be mastered.
10. This is only true for excellent teachers who have native-like fluency in the target language. Teachers with less than native-like fluency tend to rely heavily on their textbooks.

Bibliography

ASHER, J. 1969, The total physical response approach to second language learning. *Modern Language Learning* 53, 1, 3–17.

ASHER, J. J. and ADAMSKI, C. 1977, *Learning Another Language Through Actions: The Complete Teacher's Guidebook*. Los Gatos, Calif.: Sky Oak Productions.

AUSTIN, J. L. 1962, *How To Do Things With Words*. Cambridge: Harvard University Press.

BANCROFT, W. J. 1978, The Lozanov method and its American adaptations. *Modern Language Journal* 62, 4, 167–74.

BREEN, M. and CANDLIN, C. 1980, The essentials of a communicative curriculum in language teaching. *Applied Linguistics* 1, 89–112.

BROWN, P. and LEVINSON, S. 1978, Universals in language usage: politeness phenomena. In ESTHER, N. GOODY, (ed.) *Questions and Politeness: Strategies in Social Interaction*. Cambridge: Cambridge University Press.

CANALE, M. and SWAIN, M. 1979, *Communicative Approaches to Second Language Teaching and Testing*. Review and Evaluation Bulletins. Toronto: Ontario Institute for Studies in Education.

—— 1980, Theoretical bases of communicative approaches to second language teaching and testing. *Applied Linguistics* 1, 1, 1–47.

CARRELL, P. and KONNEKER, G. 1981, Politeness: Comparing native and non-native judgments. *Language Learning* 31, 17–30.

CARROLL, J. 1971, Current issues in psycholinguistics and second language teaching. *TESOL Quarterly* 5, 2, 101–14.

—— 1974, Learning theory for the classroom teacher. In G. A. JARVIS (ed.) *The Challenge of Communication* (pp. 142–5). Skokie, Ill.: National Textbook Co.

CHOMSKY, N. 1957, *Syntactic Structures*. The Hague: Mouton.

—— 1966, Linguistic Theory. *Language Teaching: Broader Contexts*. Northeast Conference on the Teaching of Foreign Languages.

CURRAN, C. A. 1976, *Counseling-Learning in Second Languages*. Apple River, Ill.: Apple River Press.

ERVIN-TRIPP, S. 1976, Is Sybil there? The structure of some American English directives. *Language in Society* 5, 25–66.

FRIES, C. C. 1945, *Teaching and Learning English as a Foreign Language.* Ann Arbor: The University of Michigan Press.

GATTEGNO, C. 1972, *Teaching Foreign Languages in Schools the Silent Way.* 2nd edn. New York: Educational Solutions.

GUMPERZ, J. J. and HYMES, D. (eds) 1964, The ethnography of communication. *American Anthropologist* 66: 6, part 2.

—— (eds) 1972, *Directions in Sociolinguistics: The Ethnography of Communication.* New York: Holt, Rinehart and Winston.

HYMES, D. 1967, The anthropology of communication. In F. DANCE (ed.) *Human Communication Theory.* New York: Holt, Rinehart and Winston.

—— 1972, Communicative competence. In J. B. PRIDE and J. HOLMES (eds) *Sociolinguistics* (pp. 269–93). Harmondsworth, England: Penguin Books.

JAKOBOVITS, L. A. 1969, Prolegomena to a theory of communicative competence. *Journal of English as a Second Language.* November.

JOHNSON, F. C. 1984, *Teaching English as a Foreign Language in the Primary School: A Communicative Approach.* Hong Kong: Educational Publishing House.

KELLY, L. G. 1969, *25 Centuries of Language Teaching.* Rowley, Mass.: Newbury House.

KRASHEN, S. D. 1981, *Second Language Acquisition and Second Language Learning.* Oxford: Pergamon.

KUHN, T. S. 1971, *The Structure of Scientific Revolutions.* Chicago: University of Chicago Press.

LEVIN, L. 1969, *Implicit and Explicit: A Synopsis of Three Parallel Experiments in Applied Linguistics Assessing Different Methods of Teaching Grammatical Structures in English as a Foreign Language.* Gothenburg: School of Education, Research Bulletin 1, University of Gothenburg.

LOZANOV, G. 1979, *Suggestology and Outlines of Suggestopedy.* New York: Gordan and Breach.

MOULTON, W. G. 1961, Linguistics and language teaching in the United States, 1940–1960. In C. MOHEMANN *et al.* (eds) *Trends in European and American Linguistics.* Utrecht: Spectrum.

MUNBY, J. 1978, *Communicative Syllabus Design.* Cambridge, NY: Cambridge University Press.

OLLER, J. and OBRECHT, D. H. 1968, Pattern drill and communicative activity: a psycholinguistic experiment. *IRAL* 6, 2, 165–72.

PAULSTON, C. B. 1970, Structural pattern drills: a classification. *Foreign Language Annals* 4, 2.

—— 1974, Linguistic and communicative competence. *TESOL Quarterly* 8–4, 347–62.

—— 1979, Communicative competence and language teaching. *Guidelines for Communication Activities.* Singapore: RELC.

—— 1981, Notional syllabuses revisited: some comments. *Applied Linguistics* 2, 1, 93–5.

PRATOR, C. 1980, In search of a method. In K. CROFT (ed.) *Readings on English as a Second Language.* Cambridge, Mass.: Winthrop.

RICHARDS, J. C. 1983, The secret life of methods. *Working Papers,* Department of English as a Second Language. University of Hawaii at Manoa, 2, 2, 1–21.

RICHARDS, J. C. and RODGERS, T. 1982, Method: approach, design, and procedure. *TESOL Quarterly* 16, 2, 153–68.

RINTELL, E. 1979, Getting your speech act together: the pragmatic ability of second language learners. *Working Papers on Bilingualism* 17, 97–106.

RIVERS, W. 1973, From linguistic competence to communicative competence. *TESOL Quarterly* 7, 1.

RUTHERFORD, W. 1968, *Modern English*. New York: Harcourt, Brace and World.

SAVIGNON, S. 1971, Study of the effect of training in communicative skills as part of a beginning college French course on student attitude and achievement in linguistic and communicative competence. Ph.D. dissertation, University of Illinois at Urbana-Champaign.

—— 1978, Teaching for communication. In E. G. JOINER and P. B. WESTPHAL (eds) *Developing Communication Skills*. Rowley, Mass.: Newbury House.

—— 1983, *Communicative Competence: Theory and Classroom Practice*. Reading, Mass.: Addison-Wesley.

SCARCELLA, R. 1979, On speaking politely in a second language. In C. YORIO, K. PERKINS and J. SCHACTER (eds) *On TESOL '79*. Washington, DC: TESOL.

SEARLE, J. 1976, A classification of illocutionary acts. *Language in Society* 5, 1–25.

STEVICK, E. W. 1980, *Teaching Languages: A Way and Ways*. Rowley, Mass.: Newbury House.

SWAIN, M. 1983, Communicative competence: some roles of comprehensible input and comprehensible output in its development. In S. GASS, and C. MADDEN (eds) *Input in Second Language Acquisitions*. Rowley, Mass.: Newbury House.

TIKUNOFF, W. J. 1983, *Compatability of the SBIF Features with Other Research on Instruction for LEP Students*. Significant Bilingual Instructional Features Study. Washington, DC: National Institute of Education and San Francisco: Far West Laboratory.

VAN EK, J. A. 1978, *The Threshold Level of Modern Language Teaching in Schools*. Longmans.

WALTERS, J. 1979, Strategies for requesting in Spanish and English. *Language Learning* 29, 277–93.

WARDHAUGH, R. 1969, TESOL: Current problems and classroom practices. *TESOL Quarterly* 3, 2.

WIDDOWSON, H. G. 1978, *Teaching Language as Communication*. London: Oxford University Press.

WILKINS, D. 1976, *Notional Syllabuses*. London: Oxford University Press.

WINITZ, H. and REEDS, J. A. 1973, Rapid acquisition of a foreign language by avoidance of speaking. *IRAL* 11, 4, 295–317.

WOLFSON, N. 1981, Compliments in cross-cultural perspective. *TESOL Quarterly* 15, 2, 117–24.

11 Linguistic Interaction, Intercultural Communication and Communicative Language Teaching

Introduction

The most obvious aspect of language learning is the learning of new words for familiar matters, the acquisition of a parallel lexicon. But we soon discover that words do not have exact equivalences and that it is difficult to give a Chinese counterpart for *privacy*. Cultural aspects of another world-view interferes with our language learning. And when it comes to actually using our newly acquired words, we find that communication is a lot more complicated than simply using words we know and understand perfectly well in the new language. Words have social as well as referential meaning, and without knowledge of the former, messages between two speakers from different cultures frequently become confused. The study of this whole area of confusion is known as intercultural communication, and for anyone who goes to live in another culture or even just wants to read about another culture, it is a subject well worth studying.

This paper deals primarily with issues in intercultural communication for students in tertiary education in China and for Chinese university students in the United States.[1] But I have also included some comments on the implications for language teaching in general in China; my Chinese students of today will become tomorrow's English teachers and teacher trainers, and some reflections on the generalizability of their experience to communicative language teaching is germane.

113

Concepts and Definitions

English as a world language

As far back as we have recorded history, we have evidence of languages used as a lingua franca,[2] i.e. as means of communication between peoples of mutually unintelligible languages. Another term frequently used is Joshua Fishman's (1971) LWC or Languages of Wider Communication. Such languages come and go as international languages, and the Western world has during this millennium seen a succession from Greek to Latin to French to English. Today more people around the world speak English as a second language than as native speakers (Fishman, Cooper & Conrad, 1977; Smith, 1976).

Having one generally accepted world language is mostly a matter of expediency and practicality. Air traffic controllers need immediate and comprehensive communication and so do sea captains. International commerce and trade would be impossible without a lingua franca. World-wide cooperation like the United Nations presupposes mutual comprehension. In one sense, it is really only during this century with advances in technology of telephone, radio, television and air travel that one can truly speak of a world language.

There are many factors which contribute to the status of a Language of Wider Communication, but one common factor is the prestige and power of its speakers. There are many bases for prestige and power but the most common are military/political and economic, and English forms no exception. The development of English as a world language can be traced to the time of World War II which ended with victory for the Allied Forces. Other major factors were ex-colonial British influence, American technological advances, and the state of the economy.

Once a nation decides that its major foreign language is to be English, it quickly develops a sizeable investment in textbooks, curriculum development, and man-power training, especially teachers, and so will be slow to change to another language. China is a perfect example of the cost and effort involved in changing a major, official LWC with the retooling of Russian teachers to English, the development of new curricula, and the concern about textbooks (which occasionally brings China into conflict with the world-wide Bern convention of copyrights). When the dust settles, Chinese students have returned from Australia, Great Britain and the United States, and the English teaching program is in place, China is likely to remain with the rest of the world in using English even after power and prestige have passed from its native speakers, just because of its enormous investment of effort and money in English as a world language. Only the future will tell what happens to English as a world language, but it is probably in place for several hundred years, and after that the world may well be learning *pu tong hua*,[3] but we, the present generation, will never know another world language than English. This has implications, both for the importance of English to China and for the objectives of language teaching.

Communicative Language Teaching (CLT)

What do we mean by communicative competence in language teaching? People mean two different things with it, and it is often confusing because it is not clear which definition they had in mind. Rivers (1973) and those who work with foreign language teaching in the United States tend to define Communicative Competence as simply linguistic interaction in the target language: 'the ability to function in a truly communicative setting; that is, in a spontaneous transaction involving one or more other persons' (Savignon, 1978: 12). People who work in ESL, on the other hand, tend to use communicative competence in Hymes' (1967: 72) sense to include not only the linguistic forms of the language but also its social rules, the knowledge of when, how, and to whom it is appropriate to use these forms. In the latter view, the objectives of language teaching are held to include the socio-cultural rules for language use, not as an added cultural component, but as an integral part of the language taught. To wit, there are rules in American English not only for forming grammatically correct wh-questions but also for the topic of questions which are admissable and socially appropriate. A Japanese banker some years ago when I was promoted to associate professor asked me how old I was to be so promoted. I simply did not answer his question because I thought it was both inappropriate and inadmissable. I told him instead that age had nothing to do with it which he, in his turn, found a very peculiar remark.

The choice of definition one chooses to work with is important and will to a considerable degree decide goals and objectives as well as syllabi and curriculum of language teaching. In the remainder of this paper I will use communicative competence to refer to the anthropological sense of socio-cultural rules for language use and use CLT primarily to refer to spontaneous oral interaction in general. The reason for this choice is that Hymes' notion of communicative competence is the key concept, not necessarily for language teaching, but certainly for dealing with intercultural communication and the confusion and misunderstandings that so often arise in such situations.

Intercultural communication

Intercultural communication is the communication between two (or more) speakers who do not share the same set of communicative competence. On a superficial level, communicative competence may simply be defined as tact and good manners, and people not sharing the same system will consider others rude and tactless. This is especially true if they are speaking the same language, but with different communicative competence rules. Black English, i.e. American Negro non-standard vernacular, has features of loudness of voice, touching behavior, and averted eye contact as a sign of respect which all differ from standard Anglo rules, and consequently such speakers risk being considered troublesome and shifty, when nothing could have been further from their intentions. Direct eye contact in standard American English signals honesty and overt dealings while in Black English it can be rude and disrespectful. American children learn to look their parents in the eye; 'Look at me when I talk to you', I have said hundreds of times to my children. They eventually learned the importance of direct eye contact, especially when they did not tell the truth but wanted to be believed, because Anglo interpretation of lack of eye contact is lack of honesty. In contrast, Black mothers admonish their children 'Don't look at me in that tone of voice!' and demand respect by averted eye contact. And consequently the white speaker interprets intended respect of black behavior as dishonesty. The basic problem is that the same set of behavior carries different meaning for the two speakers and that they are both unaware of the other set of rules.[4]

Here is another anecdote from my recent visit to China. A Canadian colleague and I travelled to Guilin with our admirable guide Heping Liu in very hot weather. Sight-seeing is thirsty business, we did not trust the water, and delighted in the excellent beer which we politely offered Heping. Heping refused, we said nothing and drank our beer, while poor Heping watched. One day Heping must have been desperate because he accepted the first offer. Only when I saw that Heping in fact liked beer, did it then occur to me to ask him whether maybe in Chinese it was not polite to accept a first offer. Indeed, it is not, and as the Chinese reader of this anecdote understands perfectly well, Heping was being modest, polite and well-behaved and had every intention of accepting the beer at the second or third offer, impressing his charges with his modesty. But Heping had not figured on North American rules which firmly say that you do not push alcoholic beverages on anyone. A person may not drink for religious reasons, he may be a reformed alcoholic, he may be allergic; whatever the reason behind the rule, you do not insist in offering alcohol. And while I certainly did not figure Heping for Mormon, Muslim or alcoholic, so unconscious and so strong are our communicative competence rules that we equally politely never made a second offer of beer to Heping who probably thought North Americans most uncouth.

When intercultural communication functions well, which it probably does most of the time, it is not problematic. It is when intercultural communication miscarries with a double misinterpretation of speakers' intention as in the previous anecdote that cross-cultural communication becomes of concern. How then do we learn to avoid misunderstandings, the basic problem in intercultural communication?

The Study of Intercultural Communication

Introduction

Intercultural communication is difficult to study. By definition, the study always involves at least one language of which the researcher is not a native speaker. But even native speakers themselves do not always know the communicative competence rules of their own language at a level where they can easily ascertain and describe them. In addition, there is a range of variability of rules from speaker to speaker; Smith's (1985) description of a wide range of rejoinders to American *thank you* surprised me, not just *you are welcome* which everyone recognizes as American (apparently calqued on Irish) but *ah ha* and *OK,* the latter which I would until recently have denied as native usage. In order to study intercultural communication, core norms of both interacting sets of communicative competence must be described and contrasted, and only segments of such descriptions exist, many of them unpublished theses (see e.g. Smith, 1985; Wolfson, 1981; Walters, 1979; Scarcella, 1979; Ervin-Tripp, 1976; Carrell & Konneker, 1981; Brown & Levinson, 1978; Apte, 1974; Morris, 1983; Schmandt, 1983; Starr, 1983).

Another difficulty lies with basic description. Pragmatics is in its infancy, and units of data and analysis are not settled. I find the work of philosophers like Austin (1962) and Searle (1976), who pioneered the study of speech act theory, of dubious value to students of English as a second language. Much more useful have been the contributions from the ethnographic study of speech use or, more simply, the ethnography of communication (Gumperz & Hymes, 1972; Saville-Troike, 1982; Sherzer & Darnell, 1972; Slobin, 1967).

Finally, there is the difficulty of data collection for rule description. Interviews and survey questionnaires can be useful but they are no substitute for the necessary and laborious process of intelligent participant-observation over a long period of time. It is only by direct exposure to the target culture speakers that any meaningful study and learning of intercultural communication can take place which aims at developing communicative competence of the target language.

Another problem in intercultural communication is the question of 'whose rules?' Chinese who are studying in Britain or the United States are sensitive from the very beginning to different 'ways of speaking', to use Hymes' phrase, in spite of their grammatically excellent English. This kind of intercultural communication should be distinguished from communication in which both speakers use English as a lingua franca on neutral ground with no particular obligation to observe cultural rules of the language they are using, as, for example, Indian and Chinese speakers do in Singapore. (Typically, the rules they use are those of their mother tongue, and we still find misunderstandings, but no one can claim the *norm*.) The same argument can be made for an American businessman in China using English, who if he wants to be successful, would be foolish to insist on only the communicative competence rules of standard American English.

Units of analysis

The three major areas for contributing units of analysis are *context, form* and *function*.

In order to come to terms with context, many scholars organize their data and analysis according to Hymes' linked concepts of speech situation, speech event and speech act. An example Hymes gives of a speech situation is a party, where a conversation constitutes a speech event, and a joke within the conversation is one of the many speech acts which take place during a conversation. It is readily seen that the speech situation will alter the social meaning of a speech act (and event as well). A bawdy joke may be appropriate in a soldiers' mess hall but it would be out of place during an academic lecture and offensive at a funeral. But note that what constitutes a bawdy joke is very likely to be culturally defined with different tolerance levels for bawdiness, different rules for who can tell them to whom, and indeed different sources of humour.

A speech situation may be non-verbal like a football game, but speech events and speech acts are governed by the rules or norms for the use of speech. A conversation, an academic lecture, a medical interview, a priest's sermon are all examples of speech events. Saville-Troike (1982), drawing on Hymes' work, outlines the major components of a communicative event:

1. The *genre*, or type of event (e.g. joke, story, lecture, greeting, conversation).
2. The *topic*, or referential focus.
3. The *purpose* or *function*, both of the event in general and in terms of the interaction goals of individual participants.
4. The *setting*, including location, time of day, season of year, and physical aspects of the situation (e.g. size of room, arrangement of furniture).
5. The *participants*, including their age, sex, ethnicity, social status, or other relevant categories, and their relationship to one another.
6. The *message form*, including both vocal and nonvocal channels, and the nature of the code which is used (e.g. which language, and which variety).
7. The *message content*, or surface level denotative references; what is communicated about.
8. The *act sequence*, or ordering of communicative/speech acts, including turn taking and overlap phenomena.
9. The *rules for interaction*, or what proprieties should be observed.
10. the *norms of interpretation*, including the common knowledge, the relevant cultural presuppositions, or shared understandings, which allow particular inferences to be drawn about what is to be taken literally, what discounted, etc. (1982: 137–8).

Speech acts is the smallest unit in this set of speech situation, event and act. It is easiest defined by examples; greeting, thanking, apologizing, requesting, asking permission, saying goodbye are just a few examples of speech acts in English and probably in most languages. The problem in intercultural communication does not lie so much in learning the proper forms of a speech act[5] as it does with learning when to use them. All my Chinese informants commented that Americans use greetings and thank yous much more than they are used to in Chinese and consequently the Americans strike them as much more polite. My Greek students have also commented on the many thank yous in American English, but rather than finding such usage polite, the Greeks found it unctuous. The point here is that the very same usage will be assigned a different social interpretation by speakers with different communicative competence, and one simply cannot appeal to logic of 'what should be'; one just has to learn and accept another way of speaking.

The Chinese informants also commented on the many apologies they hear daily in English, again unlike in Chinese. However, *excuse me* spoken by someone in the back of an elevator at a stop does not have the illocutionary force of an apology but rather means 'get out of my way so I can come out'. There is not a one-to-one relationship of form to function in speech acts, and students need to be alert to this.

By form, scholars refer to varieties of language. We have regional and social dialects which show variation in pronunciation, grammar and vocabulary, but no one controls the entire range of variation, and Chinese students should aim to learn standard English such as spoken on radio and television. We also have register variation, which refers to varieties of language which are associated with the setting rather than with the speakers and which varies along dimensions of formal/informal. The language appropriate to an informal discussion is not the language of an academic lecture and the greeting to a friend in passing is not the same as the opening of an interview with a professor. Since American students tend toward informality in social intercourse, Chinese students need to be aware of register variation, or they easily adopt an informal usage in inappropriate situations.[6]

Learning forms of a language may be hard work but the objectives are clear and there are explicit guidelines in grammatical rules, referential meanings, lists for memorization and the like. The function of language is much more difficult. There are no complete descriptions of the use people put English to although the speech act analyses we do have are typically functional descriptions. Native speakers cannot easily verbalize the rules they know behaviorally. The functional intent of the speaker may be quite different from the actual effect it has on the hearer, even between native speakers. Nevertheless, the social meaning of functional use varies between languages, and the learner must be sensitive to the social messages he may signal in his use of speech acts, in taking turns in a conversation (interrupting may be rude or polite depending on the language and culture), in choosing topics, in the use of silences, in phatic language and routines, and even in the choice of words (taboo words). The study of intercultural communication is above all the study of the functional dimension of language. Saville-Troike (1982) sums up these points:

> To claim primacy of function over form in analysis is not to deny or neglect the formal structures of communication; rather it is to require integration of function and form in analysis and description. Sentences and even longer strings of discourse are not to be dealt with as autonomous units, but as they are situated in communicative settings and patterns, and as they function in society. (Saville-Troike, 1982: 17)

Collecting data

As should be clear from the previous paragraphs, collecting data for the study of intercultural communication is a complicated affair. Rules for forms, functions, and contexts have to be collected and formulated. How is this done?

The first step is to realize that there are regularities, rules and patterns in the social interaction of English even if at first it looks like bewildering chaos to the Chinese student, and the second step is to develop strategies to discover them. People are people everywhere, and we have more in common than we differ. If social relations and their expressions seem strange, chances are that surface structure rules are different, and the easiest way to find out is to ask questions.

Anthropologists talk about participant-observation, by which they mean that the researcher lives and participates with the people to be studied and observes their behavior. For the student of intercultural communication, it means extensive social interaction with Americans, sensitivity to their ways of speaking (one can learn without approving), and a constant look-out for patterns and regularities. It was exactly noticing the break in Heping's pattern of refusing the offer of beer which enabled me to discover the Chinese rule that an initial refusal is never accepted at face value and so the offer is always repeated.

Observation in this case was not enough; it also took focused questioning of Heping to extract the rule. The easiest and probably most reliable way to find out about another culture is to ask questions of an intelligent and observant native speaker; what anthropologists call an informant. Every Chinese student in America (or England or Australia or anywhere abroad) should make an effort to find an American (or native) friend whom he trusts and feels comfortable asking 'stupid' questions. The questions of course are not stupid but you often feel that way asking them. Saville-Troike (1982) outlines some guidelines for interviewing in ethnographic fieldwork of which the first three are germane to the student of intercultural communication:

(a) Selecting reliable informants. Often the people who make themselves most readily available to an outsider are those who are marginal to the community, and may thus convey inaccurate or incomplete information and interfere with the acceptance of the researcher by other members of the group.
(b) Formulating culturally appropriate questions. This includes knowing what it is appropriate or inappropriate to ask about, why, and in what way.
(c) Developing sensitivity to signs of acceptance, discomfort, resentment, or sarcasm. Such sensitivity relates to the first two issues by contributing information or informant reliability and the appropriateness of ques-

tions, and on when an interview should be terminated. (Saville-Troike, 1982: 128).

In addition, there are the artifacts of high culture to be studied. One can learn much about language use from reading contemporary novels and plays and watching movies and television programs from the perspective of intercultural communication, keeping in mind the concepts outlined above under units of analysis.

Most difficult of all is the suspension of the deeply felt belief that our own rules of communicative competence are the only *right* rules. Now, I do think that *excuse me* is more polite than the jab of an elbow; but if I took umbrage every time I got jostled in China and took it for a personal attack or maybe drunken behavior (as it would be likely to be in the United States) I would simply poison my enjoyment and experience of China. Instead, I simply note that physical contact between strangers is permissible to gain way and think no more of it. Successful intercultural communication demands the ability to see the same piece of interaction in different patterns and configurations with, of course, different social meaning.

Implications for the English Language Classroom in China

There are fashions in language teaching (just as there are in women's clothing), which have nothing to do with experimental evidence of efficient methodology. Just now, the rage is communicative language teaching, and for once there is evidence in its favor (see e.g. Savignon, 1971). Students who are taught to communicate do better than those who are not. Common sense could probably have told us that. But the problem is that the swing of the pendulum of fashion has carried us off the middle road of good judgment and common sense, and we have gone too far. I do not believe that you can teach functional use without formal knowledge, nor do I believe that syllabi and textbooks for beginners should be organized according to functions (Paulston, 1981 — see Chapter 8, this volume). I also think that my own views of ten years ago need to be modified. I argued then for the necessity of teaching not only English but also the social meaning of the language, i.e. communicative competence in Hymes' (1972) sense. I still think that is necessary, as far as it is possible, for Chinese students who are bound for study abroad.

But more importantly, such students need to study the theoretical framework of the ethnography of communication,[7] need to develop their own tools for discovering guidelines through the potential problems of intercultural communication, need to develop strategies rather than memorizing finite items. All my Chinese informants had been warned not to ask Americans how old they were or how much money they earned, but not the principle behind it which says that different cultures allow different questions. To their surprise they discovered that not only were you allowed to ask questions, argumentative questions, in class but you were encouraged to do so, and to their amazement, that you could ask someone about his 'romantic affairs'. The point I am making is that since there exists no contrastive analysis of Chinese and English questions (British and American cultural rules differ here as well) the only feasible approach is to teach the underlying principle so that discovery procedures can be made more orderly (but see Liu, 1984; Kapp, 1983).

However, to insist in China that students with no plans of study abroad behave with English in a way that is culturally appropriate in the United States and which reflects American values sounds to me much like cultural imperialism. I now think that English belongs just as much to those who use it as a lingua franca, as an LWC, as it does to the English-speaking peoples. The use of English in China is an economic and political statement of citizens of the world, not a cultural orientation toward Britain or the United States.

Another concern applies to all communicative language teaching, not just to matters of communicative competence, and that is the matter of teacher competencies. As Richards & Rodgers (1982) point out, different methods require different roles of teachers and students. In the audiolingual method, the teacher controlled all activities, and closely tied to his textbook, he conducted the orchestra of his class. Breen & Candlin (1980) discuss the role of the teacher in a communicative approach which is to facilitate communication and act as independent participant:

> These roles imply a set of secondary roles for the teacher; first as an organizer of resources and as a resource himself, second as a guide within the classroom procedures and activities . . . A third role for the teacher is that of researcher and learner, with much to contribute in terms of appropriate knowledge and abilities, actual and observed experience of the nature of learning, and organizational capacities. (Breen & Candlin, 1980: 99)

In short, what communicative language teaching requires (much as the Direct Method did before it) in order to be effective is teachers with near-native competence in English. It is all very well to have communicative language teaching be the rage in Britain and the United States where the teachers are native speakers of English but quite another matter to export it to parts of the world which routinely use non-native speakers of English. Add to the requirement of teacher fluency in the target language, cultural values of saving face and the position of teachers in the social hierarchy (i.e. teachers command high respect and it is difficult for them to admit to ignorance), and it seems to me that a great deal of caution is needed in adopting a communicative approach in ESL in China's primary and secondary schools.

Summary

Today English is the major world language. While English spoken in the United States has its own communicative competence rules, English as an international language typically functions with the native rules of its speakers. Problems in intercultural communication usually stem from a confusion about the social meaning of interactions, not from the referential meaning of words. Chinese students who go to study English abroad need a basic knowledge of ethnography of communication in general and of English in specific. It is, however, unrealistic to expect the vast majority of Chinese students to give up their native ways of speaking in using English as an international language, and for them the referential meaning of English is an adequate and sufficient objective in second language learning.

Notes

1. I am grateful to my Chinese informants, Ding-xu Shi, Tianwei Xie, Hong Liu, Tian Ming Li, and Shou An Pan, all graduate students at the University of Pittsburgh, for their help and guidance. Any misinterpretations are of course my responsibility.
2. The term means 'language of the Franks' and was the language used in the Mediterranean during and after the Crusades for commerce and war.
3. If so, in *pin yin*. Characters would be a formidable deterrent to a world language.
4. Similar incidences are also bound to take place in China between various 'dialect' speakers, using *pu tong hua* as a lingua franca:

    . . . The fifty-odd ethnic groups in China have as many cultural patterns. Even within the dominant Han cultural traits vary from region to region. In Guangdong province, for instance, it is courteous for the guest to tap the table lightly with his forefinger and middle finger when the host is filling his wine glass. But in the north of China this will be interpreted as a sign of impatience. (Hu, 1985: 6)

5. This is not to deny the importance of learning the forms of phatic language in greetings, farewells, introductions, etc., and several of my informants expressed the opinion that they felt inadequately prepared. Rather, it is much easier to learn the formal aspects of speech acts.
6. For instance, 'Hi Paulston' may be an appropriate greeting for my son (in high school) from one of his male acquaintances, but it is totally inappropriate in greeting me.

7. I would suggest a book like Saville-Troike's (1982) *The Ethnography of Communication*. Dell Hymes is difficult to read even for native speakers. See also Condon & Yousef (1975); Samovar, Porter & Jain (1981); and Seelye (1976).

Bibliography

ALATIS, J. E. (ed.) 1970, *Bilingualism and Language Contact: Anthropological, Linguistic, Psychological and Sociological Aspects*. Washington, DC: Georgetown University Press.

APTE, M. L. 1974, 'Thank you' and South Asian languages: a comparative sociolinguistic study. *International Journal of the Sociology of Language* 3, 57–89.

AUSTIN, J. L. 1962, *How To Do Things With Words*. Cambridge: Harvard University Press.

BOCK, P. (ed.) 1970, *Culture Shock: A Reader in Modern Cultural Anthropology*. New York: Alfred Knopf.

BREEN, M. and CANDLIN, C. 1980, The essentials of a communicative curriculum in language teaching. *Applied Linguistics* 1, 89–112.

BRISLIN, R. W. (ed.) 1978, *Culture Learning*. Honolulu: University Press of Hawaii.

BRISLIN, R. W., BOCHNER, S. and LONNER, W. J. (eds) 1975, *Cross-Cultural Perspectives on Learning*. New York: John Wiley & Sons.

BROWN, P. and LEVINSON, S. 1978, Universals in language usage: politeness phenomena. In E. N. GOODY (ed.) *Questions and Politeness: Strategies in Social Interaction*. Cambridge: Cambridge University Press.

BURGER, H. 1971, *Ethno-Pedagogy: Cross-cultural Teaching Techniques*. Alberquerque: Southwestern Cooperative Educational Laboratory.

CANALE, M. and SWAIN, M. 1979, *Communicative Approaches to Second Language Teaching and Testing*. Review and Evaluation Bulletins. Toronto: Ontario Institute for Studies in Education.

—— 1980, Theoretical bases of communicative approaches to second language teaching and testing. *Applied Linguistics* 1, 1, 1–47.

CARRELL, P. and KONNEKER, G. 1981, Politeness: comparing native and non-native judgments. *Language Learning* 31, 17–30.

CHOMSKY, N. 1957, *Syntactic Structures*. The Hague: Mouton.

CONDON, J. C. 1984, *With Respect to the Japanese: A Guide for Americans*. Yarmouth, ME: Intercultural Press.

CONDON, J. C. and YOUSEF, F. 1975, *An Introduction to Intercultural Communication*. Indianapolis: Bobbs-Merrill.

EDGERTON, R. B. 1976, *Deviance: A Cross-cultural Perspective*. Menlo Park: Cummings Publishing Co.

ERVIN-TRIPP, S. 1976, Is Sybil there? The structure of some American English directives. *Language in Society* 5, 25–66.

FISHMAN, J. 1971, National languages and languages of wider communication in the developing nations. In W. H. W. WHITELY *Language Use and Social Change*. London: Oxford University Press.

FISHMAN, J., COOPER, R. L. and CONRAD, A. W. 1977, *The Spread of English: The Sociology of English as an Additional Language*. Rowley, MA: Newbury House.

GORDON, R. L. 1975, *Living in Latin America: A Case Study in Cross-Cultural Communication*. Skokie, IL: National Textbook Co.

GUMPERZ, J. J. and HYMES, D. (eds) 1972, *Directions in Sociolinguistics: The Ethnography of Communication.* New York: Holt, Rinehart and Winston.

HALL, E. 1959, *The Silent Language.* New York: Doubleday.

—— 1966, *The Hidden Dimension.* New York: Doubleday.

HU, W. 1985, Why bother about culture in ELT? Paper read at the International Symposium on the Teaching of English in the Chinese Context, Guangzhou, People's Republic of China, September 23–27.

HYMES, D. 1967, The anthropology of communication. In F. DANCE (ed.) *Human Communication Theory.* New York: Holt, Rinehart and Winston.

—— 1972, Communicative competence. In J. B. PRIDE and J. HOLMES (eds) *Sociolinguistics.* Harmondsworth, England: Penguin Books.

KAPP, R. A. 1983, *Communicating with China.* Chicago: Intercultural Press.

LADO, R. 1967, *Linguistics Across Cultures.* Ann Arbor: University of Michigan Press.

LA FORGE, P. G. 1983, *Counseling and Culture in Second Language Acquisition.* Oxford: Pergamon Press.

LANIER, A. R. 1981 (1973), *Living in the U.S.A.* Intercultural Press.

LIU, Z. 1984, *Two Years in the Melting Pot.* San Francisco: China Books.

MORRIS, D. 1983, A study of the request behavior of advanced learners of English as a Second Language. Unpublished MA thesis, University of Pittsburgh.

MUNBY, J. 1978, *Communicative Syllabus Design.* Cambridge: Cambridge University Press.

OSGOOD, C. E., MAY, W. H. and MIRON, M. S. 1975, *Cross-Cultural Universals of Affective Meaning.* Urbana, IL: University of Illinois Press.

PAULSTON, C. B. 1981, Notional syllabuses revisited: some comments. *Applied Linguistics* 2, 1, 93–5.

RICHARDS, J. C. and RODGERS, T. 1982, Method: approach, design and procedure. *TESOL Quarterly* 16, 2, 153–68.

RINTELL, E. 1979, Getting your speech act together: the pragmatic ability of second language learners. *Working Papers on Bilingualism* 17, 97–106.

RIVERS, W. 1973, From linguistic competence to communicative competence. *TESOL Quarterly* 7, 1.

SAMOVAR, L. A., PORTER, R. E. and JAIN, N. C. 1981, *Understanding Intercultural Communication.* Belmont, CA: Wadsworth.

SAVIGNON, S. 1971, Study of the effect of training in communicative skills as part of a beginning college French course on student attitude and achievement in linguistic and communicative competence. Ph.D. dissertation, University of Illinois at Urbana-Champaign.

—— 1978, Teaching for communication. In E. G. JOINER and P. B. WESTPHAL (eds) *Developing Communication Skills.* Rowley, MA: Newbury House.

—— 1983, *Communicative Competence: Theory and Classroom Practice.* Reading, MA: Addison-Wesley.

SAVILLE-TROIKE, M. 1982, *The Ethnography of Communication.* Oxford: Blackwells.

SCARCELLA, R. 1979, On speaking politely in a second language. In C. YORIO, K. PERKINS and J. SCHACHTER (eds) *On TESOL '79.* Washington, DC: TESOL.

SCHMANDT, L. 1983, A sociolinguistic analysis of leave-taking in natural speech settings. Unpublished MA thesis, University of Pittsburgh.

SEARLE, J. 1976, A classification of illocutionary acts. *Language in Society* 5, 1–25.

SEELYE, N. 1976, *Teaching Culture*. Skokie, IL: National Textbook Co.

SEWARD, G. 1958, *Clinical Studies in Culture Conflict*. New York: The Ronald Press Co.

SHERZER, J. and DARNELL, R. 1972, Outline guide for the ethnographic study of speech use. In J. J. GUMPERZ and D. HYMES (eds) *Directions in Sociolinguistics: The Ethnography of Communication*. New York: Holt, Rinehart and Winston.

SLOBIN, D. (ed.) 1967, *A Field Manual for Cross-cultural Study of the Acquisition of Communicative Competence*. Berkeley: University of California.

SMALLEY, W. A. 1963, Culture shock, language shock, and the shock of self-discovery. *Practical Anthropology* 10, 2.

SMITH, L. 1976, English as an International, Auxiliary Language. *The RELC Journal* 7, 2, 38–46.

—— 1985, A communicative approach to teaching English as an international language. *Cross Currents*.

SOONG, M. Y. E. 1985, A Study of Transfer in the Speech Act of Apologizing, Working Papers. Manoa: Department of English as a Second Language, University of Hawaii.

STARR, J. W. 1983, A study of the speech act of apologizing as performed by native speakers and advanced ESL learners. Unpublished MA thesis, University of Pittsburgh.

STEWART, E. C. 1971, *American Cultural Patterns: A Cross-Cultural Perspective*. Pittsburgh: Regional Council for International Education.

WALTERS, J. 1979, Strategies for requesting in Spanish and English. *Language Learning* 29, 277–93.

WOLFSON, N. 1981, Compliments in cross-cultural perspective. *TESOL Quarterly* 15, 2, 117–24.

12 ESL in Bilingual Education

Introduction

The objective of this paper is to identify some significant questions, features, and issues which relate to second language acquisition in a school setting, to children's language learning in the classroom. It will readily be seen that our state of knowledge is very unsatisfactory. We know surprisingly little about how children learn a second language. Barry McLaughlin (1982: 89) concludes his *Language Learning in Bilingual Instruction: Literature Review* with this caution: 'The point is that we are not at the conclusion stage but at the hypothesis stage. The quality and quantity of the research is simply not sufficient to support definitive statements.' This is probably the most important point that arises from examining the research in general, and it is one that I cannot sufficiently emphasize. We are beginning to be able to ask significant questions, to see trends and directions, but I want to make very clear that this paper should be read as an explorative discussion, not as any expounding of finite knowledge. It is my strong conviction that in the long run we only harm the children we want to help by pretending to a state of affairs which is inaccurate, however appealing.

I will write in generalities because we urgently need to be able to generalize about the practices and effects of bilingual instruction, but we should not forget that it is individual children of flesh and blood we are discussing. The joy and delight of the third grade Mexican-American boy, brutally raped some months earlier, who had finally learned to read in Senora Olga's class, is also a valid evaluation of bilingual education. My visit to her Texas classroom reminded me again that the most significant feature of bilingual education in the United States may well be that it helps ease the schooling of young children some of whom have a very rough life. Although this paper deals with second language acquisition, we need to remember that there are other matters in these children's life that are of higher importance, and that it is only as language acquisition becomes an indicator of school achievement, social success and integration, and the possibility for upward social mobility that second language learning becomes truly important.

Bilingual education in the United States takes place in a setting of language shift. However, the various groups shift at different rates. The Koreans (Kim *et al.*, 1981) and Vietnamese (Rupp, 1980) manifest a very rapid shift whereas the Navajo shows the slowest rate of shift (Lieberson & Curry, 1971: Spolsky, 1977). There really are not accurate figures for the Southwest because of continued illegal migration, but certainly shift among Hispanics is taking place (Teitelbaum, 1976). In such shift situations, language maintenance tends to become a very emotional matter as a marker of the old ethnicity, and some of this tension manifested itself in the early 1970s as a conflict between English as a Second Language (ESL) and bilingual education (BE) as well as between the perceived goals of the BE programs as promoting shift to English (transitional) or developing the mother tongue along with English (maintenance) bilingual education.

The general and unanimous first goal of most programs as perceived by the teachers is for the children to learn English and learn English well. In general I think it is much more common today to find BE administrators who are willing to settle for transitional BE than it would have been 20 years ago. As a result, there is less conflict and controversy within bilingual education as the goal orientation of the program participants comes to coincide more with the legal objectives as congress saw them.

Another consequence of what I see as an implicit shift to a transitional goal orientation is the attempt at alternatives to bilingual education, primarily ESL-programs and immersion programs. I will discuss these below, but the point I want to make here is that the goal orientation of those programs are the same as those of transitional BE, and so the programs themselves have become more acceptable than they were earlier.

The other major goal of BE programs is an affirmation of the children's cultural values and beliefs. This is in accordance with BE legislation and typically meets with little or no controversy in the school setting. I suspect this may also represent a slight shift from earlier positions. *Bilingual/ bicultural* was the slogan of the maintenance proponents but now it has become generally acceptable across the board, by Anglos as well as by bilingual teachers.

Instruction and Teaching in Bilingual Education

My impression from reading the Significant Bilingual Instructional Features Study (SBIFS) conducted by Tikunoff (1982) and his associates is that *the* most important teacher characteristic is efficient classroom management, and my own classroom experience supports that conclusion. Every-one interested in second language teaching would probably agree that one of the teacher's major roles is to structure the school environment so that the students can learn, and good classroom management does this. Good teach-ing allows for both learning and acquisition in Krashen's (1981) terms, where learning is the result of teaching while acquisition results from the stu-dent's processing of meaningful language input. Learning would include such activities as study of sound-symbol relationship, work with vocabulary cards, and fill-in-the blank exercises. Activities for second language acquisi-tion presumably are those where the focus is on the content or function of language, such as free compositions, making a shopping list for the make-believe store where the learning objectives are addition and getting correct change, as well as all those other activities which take place in English with-out focusing on form, such as the teaching of science and mathematics.

The integrative approach[1] makes certain of this acquisition phase of language development, and all the evidence is quite clear that without such a stage, i.e. language use for communication, language teaching is not very efficient (Savignon, 1971). The Canadian immersion programs were founded on the belief that unless the second language is used for teaching content matter rather than just taught as a subject, language learning will not take place (Swain & Barik, 1978; Swain & Lapkin, 1981). This is not to say that the learning stage can be ignored. Children also need the formal aspect of language learning, and presumably the failure of many ethnic children in submersion classes (regular mainstream classes in English which ignore some children's lack of knowledge of it) result from ignoring this need.

Competent student participation consists of accurate decoding and understanding, active participation, and obtaining feedback. It seems self-evident that a student cannot perform a task if s/he cannot understand the task expectations, but it is not clear which are the parts of language that second language learners must understand. Hatch (1978) documents what children learn in her *Second Language Acquisition* but not really how they do it. We do realize that the 'process is a very long, very demanding, and fre-quently frustrating one for the child' (Hatch, 1978: 12). I think children probably focus on vocabulary and then work out the semantic relationship between lexical items from their pragmatic knowledge of the real world. In any case it is clear that good teachers spend a lot of effort, their own and students', on vocabulary development.

I would like to make a few comments here on learning vocabulary and the use of mother tongue translation. It is perfectly possible to learn vocabu-lary in English without access to the native language, and children with nonstandardized mother tongues do just that. They use vocabulary cards with pictures and sometimes speech, and the teachers make games with points and prizes out of such learning. The children guess meaning from context, which is also how one learns words in the mother tongue. This is fairly easy with concrete items, except of course that one might guess wrong. When it comes to abstract items like *think,* teachers complain that it becomes much more difficult to get the meaning across, and when possible they resort to the easiest way, translation. For vocabulary acquisition, if the children know the corresponding item in their mother tongue, translation makes it an easier and probably much less frustrating task. Even in the Canadian immersion programs, there are instances of translation. I have many times heard a child ask things like: 'Comment dit-on *because* en francais?' asking for some word they needed.

But children don't know in either L1 or L2 much of the vocabulary learned in school, and then they have to work out the meaning in English with synonyms or dictionary definitions and practice in context. Translation is of no help. Probably the major advantage of subject matter taught in the L1 is that it develops the children's vocabulary knowledge of their mother tongue into that of a full-fledged functional language.

Much of what is perceived as vocabulary teaching is not that at all but teaching concepts like zero and its placement and capital letters for which the children then are taught labels. It seems self-evident that it is easier to explain the zero-concept in a language the children understand, but it is less clear that learning the label *mayuscula* is really any easier than the label *capital letter.* The Canadian immersion programs also make clear that it is perfectly possible to go directly from concept to labels in the L2 rather than the concept to L1 to L2 route, which is often done in US bilingual classroom. This is especially true in classes like geography and science which use many concrete props and so turn themselves into veritable language learning classes (Cazden, 1979; Rodriguez, 1981).

We see then that the use of L1 and L2 in the classroom is problematic for the task of second language acquisition and that a claim like 'obviously, using L1 for instruction better ensures . . . understanding task expectations' (Tikunoff, 1982: 19) is probably premature. McLaughlin comes to the same conclusion in his literature review: 'It would be premature to regard the issue (use of the first language) as settled. Most likely, decisions as to when and to what extent each of the bilingual child's two languages should be used in the classrooms depends on social, psychological, *and* linguistic factors. Some children, in some circumstances, need more support in their first language than others do' (McLaughlin, 1982: 34). And that is exactly what the successful teachers in the SBIFS (1982) case studies, actually do. The majority of their first language use during instruction in English is in translation to *individual* students who seem lost during instruction. And until we have more definite answers, that seems a practice they may as well continue.

Feedback is as important in language learning as it is in any learning in a school setting. But feedback in L2 learning may be even more important since it is often a way of clarifying and sorting input, meaningful input being at the very core of successful language learning. Let me illustrate the importance of feedback using Wagner-Gough's data on Homer (5 years 11 months), an Assyrian speaker learning English. He is playing with his friend Mark, building something with blocks.

> **Mark:** Quit making it so tall!
> **Homer:** What is this sulta! (angry voice)
> What is this sulta!
> **Mark:** Don't make it so tall!
> **Homer:** (Whispering to himself) What is this sulta?
> (Then in Assyrian: I ask what sulta is. He says sulta is something. I say there's no such thing as sulta.)
>
> (Wagner-Gough, 1978: 156)

Homer is processing *so tall* as *sulta* with consequent confusion and he actually asks for feedback (note his frustration). Mark does what most of us do when we are not understood the first time; he merely repeats. This is one instance where an instant translation would have been helpful, but Homer needs more than the meaning, he also needs to learn the correct forms. In a classroom, a good teacher would have done that for him.

In language learning, there is feedback on more than the formal aspects of language. There is also feedback on the functional use of language as communication, and many, including myself, hold that this is the more salient aspect of language acquisition. Homer knows well enough that Mark is making a mand, a request of some kind. In the classroom children get feedback on their request all day long, permission to go to the bathroom, to sharpen their pencil, to read in the library corner. Making mands that one very much wants to have approved is a highly motivating factor in language learning, and it is a legitimate question to wonder if such language learning occasions should automatically be ignored because requests are more readily accomplished in the L1. On the other hand, one certainly does not want to put some poor child through torture because he does not know how and does not dare ask permission in English to go to the bathroom. Tact and common sense will take a good teacher further than any linguistic knowledge about the role of feedback in language acquisition today because our knowledge is minimal.

Effective Second Language Instruction

Brophy's summary of effective teaching is hard to quarrel with:

> . . . learning gains are most impressive in classrooms in which students receive a great deal of instruction from and have a great deal of interaction with the teacher, especially in public lessons and recitations that are briskly paced but conducted at a difficulty level that allows consistent success. (Brophy, 1979: 747)

These teaching behaviors are likely to be equally true of second language teaching as of teaching in the mother tongue, and I know of no evidence which contradicts Brophy. However, in second language acquisition there is an additional consideration. Language is mainly acquired through social interaction, and some of the best language 'instructors' are in fact the other English-speaking students. Fry (1981)

> found that language use played an important role in social interaction and inclusion in the daily activities of classroom life. It was found that the students learned the language by being in the environment, interacting, and developing associations with English-speaking peers. As they learned more English, their interactions and association with English-speaking students increased. They also became more active and involved in the classroom. (Fry, 1981: abstract)

The findings are supported by those of Johnson (1980) who found peer tutoring and Milk (1980) who found small group settings efficient for language learning.

Mack (1981) found that interaction between English speakers and Spanish speakers in first grade was more efficient for English language acquisition than a structured ESL program. This topic should be further pursued and studied. All indications are that in the long run these mixed language classes are more of an asset for the students than a complication for the teacher, which it no doubt also is. Mack concludes her study 'that segregation of second language learners in an ESL class where all children are beginners in the language is an unwise policy' (Mack, 1981: abstract). It should be noted that Mack's comparison is between an ESL-only class and a regular monolingual class in English, not with a BE program. Nevertheless, the study addresses the problem of segregating ESL students, and this issue needs to be considered for ESL in bilingual education as well. (See the work of the Office of Educational Equity, Massachusetts Department of Education, *Two-Way Integrated Bilingual Education,* April 1990; and of its director Charles Glenn, 'How to Integrate Bilingual Education without Tracking', *The School Administrator,* May 1990: 28–31.)

The literature on second language learning is unanimous in supporting the enormous importance of *motivation* in L2 acquisition. On the whole, language learning or its absence is motivated by social forces which tend to have much stronger influence than any teaching method or program type *per se* (Paulston, 1980). One of the strongest arguments for BE lies precisely in its being able to counteract negative social forces. For example, there is little socioeconomic motivation for Amerindian children on the Navajo reservation to learn English, and they do learn more English in a bilingual program than in an all English program (Rosier & Holm, 1980). Bilingual education, however, is not a quick fix. The Navajo children in the Rosier & Holm study took six years to come up to national norms.

There are many indicators for successful BE programs. Students in BE programs have fewer behavior problems (Albino-Cordero, 1981), achieve at higher levels (Chavez, 1980; Dimas, 1981), have higher educational aspirations (Caples-Osorio, 1979), and have higher attendance and lower drop-out rates (Dimas, 1981) than students in mainstream programs. These factors are all motivational in nature, and they make a lot more sense for evaluating bilingual education than do reading scores and syntax measures. They make clear that second language acquisition is not the most important aspect of bilingual education.

But effective instruction also focuses on language development, both L1 and L2. And this brings us to the issue of ESL instruction. The integrative approach to language development is supported both by experience and by theory. The Canadian immersion programs were founded in the belief that young students will never learn a second language well unless it becomes the medium of instruction (Lambert & Tucker, 1972), and the experience so far has borne this out. There is, however, a distinction between immersion and submersion programs (Cohen & Swain, 1976). The Canadian immersion programs are maintenance programs with the instruction split half and half in French and English. The US submersion programs ignore the fact that the children do not know English and allow them to sink or swim. Most US immersion programs are misnomers who operate only in English with a combination language arts/ESL approach. It is doubtful that a program for middle-class mainstream Canadian children can successfully be adopted to the needs of children of subordinate ethnic groups in the United States.

We believe on the basis of other experience that an integrative approach is necessary for language learning at the elementary level. That belief does not necessarily invalidate ESL instruction. As a matter of fact, *any* Language Arts development in English in a bilingual program is plain and simple instruction in English as a second language. All the activities of vocabulary development in English which permeate many BE case studies are instances of successful ESL instruction. Why then are ESL and bilingual education sometimes considered mutually exclusive?

Rather than question whether an integrative approach is better than ESL instruction, one should ask whether children in a bilingual program, which of course means an integrative approach, stand to profit from a formal component in language learning. Some will answer that negatively. Terrell (1981) claims that sentences which are taught to children to illustrate rules or grammar will not help them use the rule in speech. Others reserve judgment. McLaughlin (1982) states:

> As children mature, however, they are more capable of dealing abstractly with language. Older children may profit from instruction that involve rule-isolation and attention to grammatical usage (Canale & Swain, 1980; Gadalla, 1981). There has been little research on this particular issue, but anecdotal evidence suggests that older children do make use of grammatical information and profit from instruction that focuses on grammatical usage. (McLaughlin, 1982: 30–1)

I think Terrell's position is overstated. In fact, learning to read in the mother tongue contains a multitude of rule-oriented activities, and there is evidence that children switch from a semantic language orientation to formal analysis about the time they enter school (Galambos, 1982). If children can process rule-oriented explanations in the L1, they probably can do it in the L2 as well, but as McLaughlin says, there is little research on this issue. Until such research is carried out, common sense would seem to dictate an integrative approach with a formal ESL-component, a practice which is prevalent among effective teachers.

There is also the question whether a modified language arts program for ESL purposes in a monolingual English program can substitute for bilingual education. The answer to that question is the core argument for the BE movement in the United States. This paper is not the place for an exhaustive answer, and the issue is more complicated than we thought ten years ago. Baker & deKanter (1981) in their much discussed report argue for an ESL approach on the basis of evaluative data from BE programs. I have argued repeatedly that one cannot just examine the educational programs but that one must also take into account the social conditions (Paulston, 1975, 1980).

It seems, that in social circumstances which do not favor rapid language shift, children from subordinate ethnic groups at the lower rungs of the social structure in fact do better in bilingual programs. Swain & Cummins (1979) also support the same argument but on the basis of linguistic factors. Cummins claims that the support of the child's first language is needed for effective L2 acquisition and socio-cognitive growth (Cummins, 1976, 1982).

Methods for Teaching ESL

I was surprised to find some 20 teachers at a workshop in Texas assure me unanimously that audio-lingual techniques, such as choral substitution, repetition, and transformation drills, work in the classroom and that the children learn from them. Although I find it very surprising that doing mechanical substitution drills with elementary school children would work, I am loathe to contradict the judgment of experienced classroom teachers. We know very little about language teaching methodology at the elementary level. (For practical considerations, see Pialorsi, 1974; Saville-Troike, 1976; von Maltitz, 1975.)

At the adult level (or post-puberty or post-critical period) there is general agreement on a communicative approach to language teaching (Canale & Swain, 1979) with the major argument that the focus of language teaching should be on language use rather than on language form. This is of course what happens in a bilingual education program but it also can (and I would add should) happen in a good ESL program (Murphy, 1978). In my opinion the ESL component of BE programs has been seriously neglected. When children come from multiple language backgrounds, it is not possible to implement bilingual programs of instruction. At such times, a good ESL program is a lot more helpful than a regular program (Scudder, 1979).

The question of age also influences preferred methods of L2 teaching. Scholars do not agree on critical period issues, but adults (past puberty) seem in some regards to learn an L2 differently than children. In his study of the impact of BE programs, Huang (1980) found that the majority of high school teachers favored ESL programs over BE programs in helping high school students with limited English proficiency improve English language skills. There has been an unfortunate tendency among some BE proponents to categorically criticize an ESL approach, but such criticism may be premature as ESL may be more effective than it has been given credit for.

Conclusion

Most BE program evaluation research compares BE programs with regular, unmodified monolingual programs. I suspect that this dearth of research is founded on ideological grounds. Many BE proponents regard ESL with misgivings. I would expect that a good ESL program, with a bilingual teacher, who code-alternated in English and the children's L1 for purposes of explanation, would be quite efficient for English learning purposes. That is after all how children in Europe learn English as a foreign language. But we don't know and until we know more about an ESL approach, we need to be judicious in our conclusions. We gain nothing with unsupportable claims.

Note

1. The integrative approach is the term used in the SBIF study for methods of teaching in BE classrooms which have been identified as academically excellent.

   In summary, the description of instruction presented here for producing the two major goals of bilingual education for NES/LES — attainment of English language proficiency and concurrent growth in academic skills attainment — specifies three underlying principles of effectiveness.

   First, classroom instruction for acquiring English-language proficiency and academic skills is an interactive process, the component pieces of which cannot be separated operationally. Thus, it is not productive to continue to use only oral English-language proficiency as a performance determiner for identifying NES/LES. Instead, operational measures of *functional proficiency* must be developed which incorporate understanding both English-language proficiency and competent participation in classroom instructional activity as described here.

   Second, because the primary medium of instruction is language, some L1 must be used for instruction if NES/LES are to be ensured of understanding the intent of instruction and therefore be enabled to participate competently in instructional activity. Only when a child's native language is used can one be relatively certain that communication can result.

   Third, the role of the bilingual teacher in mediating effective instruction is critical. It is clear that use of both L1 and L2 are necessary, that a focus on language-development is required throughout instruction, and that use of cues from a NES/LES culture contribute significantly to effective bilingual instruction.

References

ALBINO-CORDERO, H. P. 1981, An investigation of the effects of bilingual and non-bilingual school programs on pupil adjustment. Unpublished doctoral dissertation, University of Connecticut.

BAKER, K. A. and DEKANTER, A. A. 1981, *Effectiveness of Bilingual Education: A Review of the Literature*. Technical Analysis Report Series, US Department of Education.

BROPHY, J. E. 1979, Teacher behavior and its effect. *Journal of Teacher Education* 71, 733–50.

CANALE, M. and SWAIN, M. 1979, *Communicative Approaches to Second Language Teaching and Testing*. Ontario: Ministry of Education.

—— 1980, Theoretical bases of communicative approaches to second language teaching and testing. *Applied Linguistics* 1, 1, 1–47.

CAPLES-OSORIA, R. W. 1979, Educational aspirations of selected Mexican American school children enrolled in bilingual education. Unpublished doctoral dissertion, Texas A & M University.

CAZDEN, C. 1979, Curriculum/language contents for bilingual education. In *Language Development in a Bilingual Setting*. Pomona, Ca.: National Multilingual Multicultural Material Development Center, California State Polytechnic University.

CHAVEZ, R. C. 1980, A study of students' perception in bilingual/bicultural classroom climates and non-bilingual classroom climates. Unpublished doctoral dissertation, New Mexico State University.

COHEN, A. and SWAIN, M. 1976, Bilingual education: the immersion model in the North American context. *TESOL Quarterly* 10, 1, 45–53.

CUMMINS, J. 1976. The influence of bilingualism on cognitive growth: a synthesis of research findings and explanatory hypothesis. Working Papers on Bilingualism, No. 9, 1–43.

—— 1982, Linguistic interdependence among Japanese and Vietnamese immigrant students. In C. RIVERA (ed.) *The Measurement of Communicative Proficiency: Models & Applications*. Washington, DC: Center for Applied Linguistics.

DIMAS, W. A. 1981, The relative effectiveness of the Title VII bilingual program and regular mainstream program in Trenton as revealed by the students' grade point averages (QPA), attendance records and drop-out rates. Unpublished doctoral dissertation, Rutgers University.

FRY, J. J. S. 1981, English language acquisition through social interaction in classrooms in which children speak various languages. Unpublished doctoral dissertion, Michigan State University.

GADALLA, B. J. 1981, Language acquisition research and the language teacher. *Studies in Second Language Acquisition* 4, 60–9.

GALAMBOS, S. J. 1983, Development of metalinguistics awareness in bilingual and monolingual children. Lecture, University of Pittsburgh.

GLENN, C. 1990, How to integrate bilingual education without tracking. *The School Administrator* May 28–31.

HATCH, E. M. 1978, *Second Language Acquisition*. Rowley, Mass.: Newbury House.

HUANG, B-D. 1980, The impact of bilingual–bicultural education programs on an urban high school: a descriptive case study. Unpublished doctoral dissertation, Columbia University Teachers College.

JOHNSON, D. M. 1980, Peer tutoring, social interaction, and the acquisition of English as a second language by Spanish-speaking elementary school children. Unpublished doctoral dissertation, Stanford University.

KIM, K. K-O, LEE, K. and KIM, T-Y, 1981, *Korean Americans in Los Angeles: Their Concerns and Language Maintenance*. Los Alamitos, Ca.: National Center for Bilingual Research.

KRASHEN, S. 1981, *Second Language Acquisition and Second Language Learning*. Elmsford, NY: Pergamon Press.

LAMBERT, W. and TUCKER, R. 1972, *Bilingual Education of Children: The St. Lambert Experiment*. Rowley, Mass.: Newbury House.

LIEBERSON, S. and CURRY, T. J. 1971, Language shift in the United States: some demographic clues. *International Migration Review* 5, 125–37.

McLAUGHLIN, D. 1982, *Language Learning in Bilingual Instruction: Literature Review*. Manuscript, University of California at Sta Cruz.

MACK, M. 1981, The effect of a curriculum designed to improve the self-concept and English oral language skills of Spanish speaking migrant children in first grade. Unpublished doctoral dissertation, University of Florida.

MILK, R. D. 1980, Variation in language use patterns cross different group settings in two bilingual second grade classrooms. Unpublished doctoral dissertation, Stanford University.

MURPHY, B. J. 1978, The identification of the components requisite for the teaching of English to primary school Navajo students: guidelines for English as a second language in Navajo/English bilingual education. Unpublished doctoral dissertation. University of Massachusetts.

PAULSTON, C. B. 1975, Ethnic relations and bilingual education: accounting for contradictory data. In R. TROIKE and N. MODIANO (eds) *Proceedings of the First Inter-American Conference on Bilingual Education*. Arlington, VA.: Center for Applied Linguistics.

—— 1980, *Bilingual Education: Theories and Issues*. Rowley, Mass.: Newbury House.

PIALORSI, F. 1974, *Teaching the Bilingual*. Tucson: University of Arizona Press.

RODRIGUEZ, I. Z. 1981, An inquiry approach to science/language teaching and the development of classification and oral communication skills of Mexican American bilingual children in the third grade. Unpublished doctoral dissertation, University of Texas at Austin.

ROSIER, P. and HOLM, W. 1980, *The Rock Point Experience: A Longitudinal Study of a Navajo School Program*. Washington, DC: Center for Applied Linguistics.

RUPP, J. H. 1980, Cerebral language dominance in Vietnamese-English bilingual children. Unpublished doctoral dissertation, University of New Mexico.

SAVIGNON, S. 1971, Study of the effect of training in communicative skills as part of a beginning college French course on student attitude and achievement in linguistic and communicative competence. Unpublished Ph.D. dissertation, University of Illinois at Urbana, Champaign.

SAVILLE-TROIKE, M. 1976, *Foundations for Teaching English as a Second Language: Theory and Method for Multicultural Education*. Englewood Cliffs, NJ: Prentice-Hall.

SBIFS, 1982, *Significant Bilingual Instructional Features Study. Case Studies*. San Francisco: Far West Laboratory for Educational Research and Development.

SCUDDER, B. E. T. 1979, A comparative study of the effects of the use of a diagnostic prescriptive approach versus a tutorial approach to the teaching of English to non-English speaking elementary school children in a large urban school district in Colorado. Unpublished doctoral dissertation, University of Colorado at Boulder.

SPOLSKY, B. 1977, American Indian bilingual education. *International Journal of the Sociology of Language* 14.

SWAIN, M. and BARIK, H. 1978, Bilingual education in Canada: French and English. In B. SPOLSKY and R. COOPER (eds) *Case Studies in Bilingual Education*. Rowley, Mass.: Newbury House.

SWAIN, M. and CUMMINS, J. 1979, Bilingualism, cognitive functioning and education. *Language Teaching and Linguistics* Abstracts, 12, 1, 4–18.

SWAIN, M. and LAPKIN, S. 1981, *Bilingual Education in Ontario: A Decade of Research*. Ontario: Ministry of Education.

TEITELBAUM, H. 1976, Assessing bilingualism in elementary school children. Unpublished doctoral dissertation, University of New Mexico.

TERRELL, T. D. 1981, The natural approach in bilingual education. In *Schooling and Language Minority Students: A Theoretical Framework*. Los Angeles: Evaluation, Dissemination and Assessment Center, California State University.

TIKUNOFF, W. J. 1982, An emerging description of successful bilingual instruction: an executive summary of Part I of the SBIF descriptive study. Manuscript.

VON MALTITZ, F. W. 1975, *Living and Learning in Two Languages: Bilingual–Bicultural Education in the United States*. New York: McGraw-Hill.

WAGNER-GOUGH, J. 1978, Excerpts from comparative studies in second language learning. In E. M. HATCH (ed.) *Second Language Acquisition* (pp. 155–71). Rowley, Mass.: Newbury House.

Index

DATE DUE

SEP 2 5 2000			
OCT 0 1 2000			
OCT 1 0 2000			
NOV 2 2 2000			
GAYLORD			PRINTED IN U.S.A.